Y2K LESSONS LEARNED

A Guide to *Better* Information Technology Management

D1569666

Y2K LESSONS LEARNED

A Guide to *Better* Information Technology Management

TIMOTHY BRAITHWAITE

JOHN WILEY & SONS, INC.

New York • Chichester • Weinheim • Brisbane • Toronto • Singapore

Library of Congress Cataloging-in-Publication Data

Braithwaite, Timothy, 1942–
    Y2K lessons learned : a guide to better information technology management / Timothy Braithwaite.
        p. cm.
    ISBN 0-471-37308-7 (paper)
    1. Year 2000 date conversion (Computer networks)   2. Information technology.
    I. Title.
QA76.76.S64 B74 2000
005.1′6—dc21

                                                            00-025725

Printed in the United States of America.

10 9 8 7 6 5 4 3 2 1

To B. G. Braithwaite
1914–1999

CONTENTS

CONTENTS

x

ABOUT THE AUTHOR

Timothy B. Braithwaite has more than 30 years of experience in all aspects of automated data processing, communications, and information systems management. Currently director of Information Assurance Programs for AverStar, Inc., he has worked the last four years on Y2K compliance issues. Prior to that he has managed data centers, software development projects, system planning and budgeting organizations, and has extensive experience in computer acquisition activities. His pioneering work in computer systems security and privacy resulted in his appointment to the Privacy Protection Study Commission in 1976 and his recruitment to be the first systems security officer for the Social Security Administration in 1978. He has a master's degree in technology management from American University and a bachelor of science degree in business administration from Rockhurst College. He is the author of *Information Service Excellence Through TQM* (Quality Press, 1994), *The Power of IT: Maximizing Your Technology Investment* (Quality Press, 1996), and *Evaluating the Year 2000 Project: A Management Guide for Determining Reasonable Care* (John Wiley & Sons, 1998).

PREFACE

Those who cannot remember the past
are condemned to repeat it.
George Santayana

CONGRATULATIONS SEEM TO BE IN ORDER

The Y2K worldwide computing crisis, arising from a largely preventable problem, appears to have been averted. This happened as a result of a great deal of cooperation, presidential and CEO leadership, international mobilization, the exhaustive efforts of innumerable people, and the expenditure, in the United States alone, of over $100 billion. Whether, of course, crisis management is the desirable model for insuring the success of future information technology (IT) undertakings is questionable. A more effective method is the preventive approach that this book addresses in detail.

ABOUT THIS BOOK

This book will no doubt be one of many to attempt a postmortem of the Y2K experience. This book will chronicle those IT industry conditions and deficient system development and management practices that created not only the Y2K crisis, but also those many other IT problems with which most organizations are all too familiar. Unless taken seriously and acted on, these conditions and deficiencies will continue to plague all future IT endeavors.

Specific corporate IT management recommendations and system development "best practices" are suggested that could assist in preventing similar problems in the future. Many of these suggestions require executive level participation in IT decision making. This book also addresses the juggling act required of organizations that seek to benefit from new technology while managing risk and uncertainty. Four management review guides are provided for this purpose. When used, these guides can help direct the conscious evolution of IT in support of business goals.

Y2K: AN UNFINISHED STORY

Before proceeding, however, certain accusations surfacing in the immediate aftermath of the relatively uneventful January 1st rollover need to be addressed and explored for validity.

First, it is accused that Y2K was a scam foisted on the unsuspecting community of information-technology users. It has been suggested that unscrupulous IT vendors and consultants created a hypothetical problem and hyped it beyond its true importance in order to create work and wealth for themselves. To give credence to such accusations is to, by inference, accuse sophisticated executive management at such corporations as Citibank and AT&T of incompetence, or worse. No corporation spends $900 million (Citibank) and $500 million (AT&T) on a hyped hypothetical problem. To be sure, some of the monies associated with Y2K were probably misdirected, exaggerated, wasted, or even spent on non-Y2K activities, but not $100 billion.

An early argument advanced to support the accusation of scam centered on the apparent fact that countries and businesses that spent little or nothing on Y2K appear to be doing as well as those that spent heavily and were experiencing no greater number of date-related problems. To assist in making some sense of this seemingly powerful proof, four categories of IT systems and their related business settings likely to be operating in any given country or company need to be identified. The following system categories, based on their intrinsic technical vulnerability to the Y2K problem, were catalogued by the Institute of Electrical and Electronics Engineers (IEEE).

1. *Physical Control Systems* are those that control physical things and processes, such as power generation and distribution, water treatment and distribution, phones, airplanes, elevators, traffic lights, etc. These are the systems where the dreaded embedded chip failures were most anticipated. These systems, however, are well engineered and better understood, better tested under stress, and are often designed with redundancy built-in. Such systems have always had a

good degree of management attention and investment because in many cases these systems actually constitute the business.

2. *Primary Production Systems of an On-Line Transaction Processing (OLTP) Systems* such as ATM and e-commerce processing systems were not on the vulnerability list because of the highly integrated and frequently customized nature of hardware and software components and their convergence. Also, OLTP systems are often not engineered with sufficient redundancy and not adequately stress tested.

3. *Support Systems* are those that monitor and detect faults, schedule maintenance, automatically order parts, etc., and to some extent manage primary production (OLTP) systems for efficiency and safety. Such systems are not overly complex and are generally well understood. They are not as well engineered as OLTP systems, are not stress tested, and have limited redundancy.

   Note that Y2K problems with Support Systems would not appear immediately but would surface only after a preprogrammed time interval has elapsed. In other words, these categories of systems can be deemed safe only after all time intervals with 1999-initiated start times have been successfully compared to a post-2000 stop time and all computations and resulting programmed actions have been carried out.

   Also note that a combination of category 1, 2, and 3 systems, operating at different companies, constitute and support the just-in-time (JIT) business model on which many corporations depend.

4. *Administrative and Accounting (A&A) Systems* are heavily date dependent and support the general economic activities of organizations such as purchasing, order processing, invoicing, accounting, human resources, payroll, benefit calculations, tax reporting, etc. These systems are virtually all software and after years of modifications and extensions are extremely complex. A&A systems run on daily, weekly, monthly, quarterly, semi-annually, and annual cycles; meaning that an entire software portfolio may not execute under actual year 2000 conditions until next December. These systems typically provide the data against which "what if" queries are run and are also used for "data warehousing" activities. A&A systems are oftentimes very large, highly interconnected with many shared data sources, and are often composed of heterogeneous technologies of

diverse vendors, models, and age. As a whole, such systems are not generally well understood due to a lack of documentation. These systems present virtually the worst-case scenario for all Y2K-related risk factors and, because they have historically been reviewed as a cost center, they have received relatively little management attention and investment.

Category 4 system problems, due to Y2K, will not be immediately visible outside an organization since they are generally "backroom" processes that can be carefully screened. Failures with A&A systems will not result in press coverage unless errors escape an organization's quality control procedures and adversely impact a business partner or customer.

But A&A problems due to Y2K may cause great, unexpected internal turmoil as systems progress through their calendar year 2000 processing cycles. Only the readers of this book will know whether such conditions have occurred in their organization. Although failures with A&A systems may be difficult to link to Y2K date-processing problems, this does lessen the impact. An increase in problems over last year will be the telltale sign.

The existence of these four categories of systems, with their intrinsic Y2K vulnerabilities, provide a partial answer to the accusation that non-spenders are faring as well as heavy spenders. It seems likely that there are two possibilities with regard to Physical Control Systems, Primary Production Systems, and their Support Systems. First, since these are highly visible and liability-prone systems providing the basic infrastructures of a nation and corporations, they were in fact rigorously remediated and tested. Due diligence would have demanded nothing less. Secondly, such systems in developing nations and less IT-intensive businesses do not even exist, at least to the degree of sophistication that they do in developed nations and large corporations. In which case, there were no reported problems simply because there was nothing to fail that could not be handled manually. Only in more advanced and sophisticated systems has the progressive elimination of the human override element become a desired cost-cutting design goal. Such systems had to be fixed, whereas less sophisticated systems in developing nations or less IT-intensive businesses retained the luxury of the human override and workaround.

With regard to category 4 or the A&A systems, these were always viewed by Y2K practitioners as the most troublesome for the reasons cited. According to the IEEE, if we are to have major damage to the economy and business it will come from the A&A systems and those business and governmental activities dependent on them. This will take time and have long-term impacts on the economy, but particulars of those impacts are hard to decipher in early 2000. Such A&A system problems will also affect nonspenders in due course and it is heartily hoped that they can muddle through. To the extent that Y2K spenders remediated their A&A systems they will be less likely to experience problems. Again, this is the unfolding part of the unfinished Y2K story as A&A systems complete their yearly cycles of processing.

There has also been an accusation that those addressing their perceived vulnerabilities spent too much money on Y2K. In response, it can only be pointed out that "reasonable" men and women, upon analysis, practiced responsible risk management and perhaps erred on the side of caution. Again, it is a fact that developed nations and highly IT-intensive businesses had more at risk because of their great dependence on systems built to reduce the labor-intensive (i.e., potential human override) nature of their work processes.

WHAT OF THE HUMAN ELEMENT

In a January 10th editorial by Tim Wilson of *Internet Week,* appears the following: "Sometimes I wonder why anybody works in the IT Department. If computers fail, you get yelled at. If Internet or dial-up connections fail you get yelled at. And now, if everything works well, you really get yelled at."

Whether the Y2K "bug" stays defeated in the months ahead, or is merely replaced by another crisis, it is clear that future successful uses of IT will become a complex technical and *social* undertaking. The apparent fact that many users of IT perceive the IT industry and IT workers with such suspicion and antipathy means that much IT industry/user mutual respect work lies ahead. This essential work can begin by carefully identifying and exploring the lessons to be learned from the Y2K experience because Y2K, as a discrete event, presents a unique opportunity to influence the evolutionary path of IT. Now is the time to condemn the bad practices and evaluate the questionable ones that produced the Y2K crisis. It is also the time to inventory those practices that allowed disaster to be averted.

Y2K has presented the IT industry and the user community with a teachable moment. Let us seize that moment and jointly determine an IT business management model for responsible computing.

Y2K LESSONS LEARNED

A Guide to *Better* Information
Technology Management

1

TECHNOLOGY-BASED ISSUES THAT HAVE CONTRIBUTED TO THE Y2K PROBLEM

INTRODUCTION

At the heart of the Y2K experience lie many fundamental conditions that, for years, have plagued the uses of information technology (IT). A short summary of conditions would include the following:

- Explosive growth of the technology
- Failure to acknowledge limitations inherent to applications of the technology
- Difficulty in managing the "creeping" complexity of evolving applications
- Lack of executive involvement in critical IT decisions
- The slow emergence of standards
- Chronic shortage of trained, experienced IT personnel
- Failure to adopt or enforce those standards that did emerge
- Lack of critical thinking regarding IT and its applications
- Failure to manage risk
- Failure to enforce discipline in the development of systems and their delivery
- Failure to insist on quality as a primary design criterion
- Failure to fund operations and maintenance adequately

1

- Lack of accountability
- Failure to give Murphy's Law its due

Murphy's Law states that "whatever can go wrong will go wrong." Then, of course, there is the corollary that states "Murphy was an optimist." Both statements and the conditions just listed would seem to indicate that IT applications are a high-risk undertaking. Yet, in their rush to use new technologies, organizations often have ignored risk and have proceeded to implementation with breakneck speed.

The conditions just listed, and many others that shall be explored, have conspired to place business, government, society, and individuals in positions of dependence on many systems that are fundamentally unstable, unreliable, insecure, and very difficult to administer and maintain. The Y2K difficulties experienced by organizations provide ample evidence of the truth of this statement. How else could an entire industry (IT) have experienced such expense dealing with a seemingly simple problem except that the actual problem stemmed not from the date correction task itself but from the challenge of managing such a project in light of the underlying conditions just mentioned?

It is tempting to wonder about the existence of other technology-based problems awaiting us and to ask if these technologies are better managed. But then we would soon realize that IT is at the core of all contemporary technologies and would already know the answer. With infrastructure applications of great importance and high risk, IT does seem to be better managed; but these applications are the exception. With many business applications, IT risks are rarely assessed and rarely mitigated through stringent development and testing techniques. With most applications, when analysis and thinking time is asked for, the rejoiner is all too often "Why isn't someone coding?"

If something as simple as a date change and two digits could cause this much disruption, what harm could an unanticipated and truly complex technology problem do to a dependent company or society?

Answers lie not in throttling future technological advances but in adopting analytic techniques and management methods that account for risk and require the development and delivery of systems of much higher reliability and improved quality.

The good news is that these analytic techniques and management methods already exist and have long been available to managers of IT. In fairness, often the problem has been the inability of the conscientious IT manager to overcome the underlying conditions and successfully argue against the "highly marketed" benefits of the too-rapid adoption, development, and delivery of systems of questionable reliability and maintainability. Information technology processing is a complex business with tentacles extending into all parts of the enterprise. Only by understanding the issues surrounding mistakes of the past 30 years can executives hope not to repeat the same mistakes following the year 2000.

CAPABILITIES OF IT VS. LIMITATIONS

In the early days of my career, following a five-year tour of duty as a Data Automation officer in the U.S. Air Force, I was selected in 1968 to be a member of the faculty of a pioneering organization designated the Department of Defense Computer Institute. The institute had been chartered in the middle 1960s by the secretary of defense to instruct general and flag officers and senior civilian executives in the capabilities and limitations of computers and the application of automation. It was recognized at the secretary's level, and through the urgings of such people as then Captain Grace Hooper, USN, and Dr. Carl Hammer of UNIVAC and others, that senior government officials needed to be grounded in what computers realistically could be expected to accomplish. With this understanding, they would then be equipped to make intelligent decisions concerning this new technology. It was recognized, early on, by the sponsors of the institute that nontechnical managers and executives could be susceptible to the unfounded claims of proponents of the fledgling technology and be taken advantage of. Of course, the only people capable of carrying out such marketing activities would be those well versed in the technology and with business development as their guiding principle. Executives, it was thought, needed to be educated and familiar enough with computer basics to be able to determine fact from at least gross fiction. To accomplish this end, the course of instruction for senior executives conveyed the following critical concepts.

Concept 1: Computers Are Exacting

At the institute this concept was driven home to the executives by their actual programming of computers using the BASIC language. This demonstrated that although computers are amazing machines, they are extremely demanding in their use. Following the Y2K experience, this realization has renewed meaning. Programming at the institute required the generation of a logical flow chart, the development of a means to test the program, introduction of the program language statements to the computer, and initiation of the computer to run the program. Those executives learned a great deal about the demanding nature of computers and experienced the valuable insight that computers do exactly what they are instructed to do, nothing more and nothing less.

Today an introduction to computing for senior executives would likely have them executing a preprogrammed routine where they are invoking, through an icon and a mouse click, thousands of lines of fully tested code. Such an exercise illustrates the capabilities of the computer but nothing of its inherent limitations. The computer in these situations is generally depicted as a "thinking machine," not as the "instruction-following" device it actually is.

Concept 2: Computers Do Some Things Well, Other Things Not So Well

In other words, based on the executives' newfound appreciation for the demanding nature of the computer came the realization that the division of labor in an organization had to be carefully allocated between computers and people. Exhibit 1.1 illustrates this division of tasks.

While seeming to be obvious, the potential for misassigning tasks between people and computers may be at the bottom of much of the dissatisfaction with IT when viewed by those who work with the computer. For example, many people feel dread when talking to an automated phone answering system. Clearly, any rational executive desiring not to irritate customers will see the potential for business damage by this common mismatch between computer and people tasking. To be sure, there are situations well suited to the automated answering system, but the risk to customer relations would seem to indicate that great care be taken, by aware executives, with even this seemingly mundane decision concerning the use of IT.

Exhibit 1.1 Division of Work between People and Computers

Elements of Work That People do Well:	Tasks That Computers Perform as Instructed:
Taking Physical Action	Capturing Data
Creative Thinking	Transmitting Data
Decision Making	Storing/Retrieving
Communicating Ideas	Manipulating
Recognizing Patterns	Displaying
Processing Information	

Dissatisfaction with automated systems that have been imposed on operational business settings has been running consistently high since surveys were first taken. Exhibit 1.2 illustrates the impact of IT systems on organizations and whether, from the perspective of those working with the system on a daily basis, the implementation was a success, a marginal success, or a failure.

This perspective is crucial for executives to understand because it illustrates the practical business implications of not being involved in the next century's IT decision-making process. While there are several contributing explanations for the dismal showing depicted in the exhibit, one critical reason may be that the limitations of computers and their applications are not taken fully into account before system decisions are made and implemented.

The reality of Exhibit 1.2 has just been experienced again in the fact that some Y2K solutions have failed in the workplace or were just marginally acceptable.

Concept 3: Rigorous Methods Are Needed to Manage Demanding Technologies

Because of the unforgiving nature of computers, the ease with which they can be misapplied, and the difficulty in achieving successful implementations, the institute's executive students were introduced to the solution: the discipline provided by a systematic process for systems development. Exhibit 1.3 depicts a generic system development process (SDP).

Exhibit 1.2   Success Rates in Information Technology Application

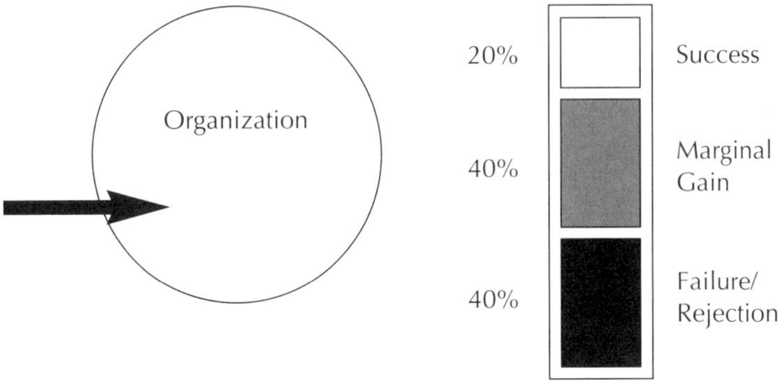

Source: Adapted from Ken Eason, *Information Technology and Organizational Change* (London: Taylor & Francis, 1988), 12, 33, 55.

The systems development process, in whatever representation, provides the vehicle and structure needed to address the challenge of successfully applying IT to a business opportunity or to solve a problem. The SDP is accepted as the fundamental work-process of system and software developers. It is taught in all university programs and is available in many different commercially marketed versions. Whether the steps are performed manually or are supported by automated tools, it is the thought process that is important. This thought process and the discipline are all too easily abandoned in the rush to get something into the hands of the customer. System developers, in the aftermath of Y2K, may well find that some basic decisions have been made for them. For example, when it comes to delivering automated systems, software, and services, the marketplace may turn away from rewarding the *first* to rewarding the *best*. If so, IT executives must use the SDP, and other suggestions to be found in this book, to get as close to being *first* as possible while knowing they will be rewarded, in the long run, only by being *best*.

COMPLEXITY OF SOFTWARE AND SYSTEMS

The new international airport at Denver was to be a marvel of modern engineering. It was designed to land three jets simultaneously in inclement

Exhibit 1.3 Systems Development Proces

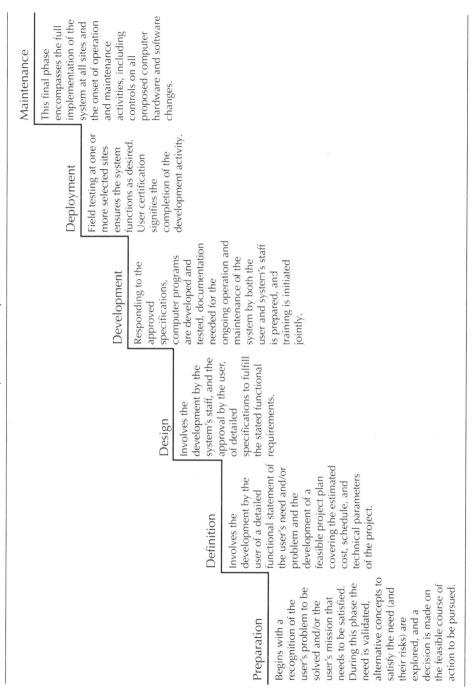

Preparation

Begins with a recognition of the user's problem to be solved and/or the user's mission that needs to be satisfied. During this phase the need is validated, alternative concepts to satisfy the need (and their risks) are explored, and a decision is made on the feasible course of action to be pursued.

Definition

Involves the development by the user of a detailed functional statement of the user's need and/or problem and the development of a feasible project plan covering the estimated cost, schedule, and technical parameters of the project.

Design

Involves the development by the system's staff, and the approval by the user, of detailed specifications to fulfill the stated functional requirements.

Development

Responding to the approved specifications, computer programs are developed and tested, documentation needed for the ongoing operation and maintenance of the system by both the user and system's staff is prepared, and training is initiated jointly.

Deployment

Field testing at one or more selected sites ensures the system functions as desired. User certification signifies the completion of the development activity.

Maintenance

This final phase encompasses the full implementation of the system at all sites and the onset of operation and maintenance activities, including controls on all proposed computer hardware and software changes.

weather. Underground, the baggage-handling system delivered luggage among counters, gates, and baggage claim areas for 20-plus different airlines. This system was dependent on 100 networked computers, 400 radio transmitters and receivers, over 50 bar code scanners, and some 5,000 electric eyes. At least that was the way it was supposed to be. After an expenditure of over $193 million and delay of almost a year that threatened the planners with bankruptcy, the system was finally deemed complete enough, with workarounds, to permit the opening of the airport.

The experience just related is notable only for the publicity it received. Software veterans know that at least two of every eight new large-scale systems get canceled and that the remaining six never fully meet their anticipated promise, these numbers reflect the technology reason for the truth of Exhibit 1.2. Additionally, the average software project overshoots its schedule and budget by half. Larger projects do even worse. These statistics have been proven again in that many Y2K projects were also over budget, late, or scaled down to appear successful.

Complexity and size are the two most common denominators when describing the world's crisis with software. In a mere 35 years, project complexity has progressed from approximately 1 million lines of coded instructions for NASA's Project Mercury, to 50 million lines for the space shuttle, to an estimated 100 million lines for the space station. By comparison, the Windows 95 operating system, with all functions, came in at close to 25 million lines of instructions and NT 2000 is variously estimated to be between 40 and 50 million lines of code. Today the amount of computer code in consumer products is doubling every two years or less. Products used every day may contain thousands of lines of coded instructions, usually in the form of embedded chips. Manufacturing processes may have many millions of coded instructions in the form of Programmable Logic Controllers (PLCs).

The initial estimates of the Y2K date computing problem focused on traditional software with lines of written coded instructions as the important measure of the systems that operate businesses and government. Since hundreds of different programming languages have been used to generate these instructions, a leveling measure known as a function point has been used to summarize the effort. The function point metric takes into account a great many variables concerning the programming language and characteristics of the application being programmed. Function point metrics originated within IBM during the 1970s and have become the most widely used measure for project estimation in the software world. For an application being described by function points, an easy rule of thumb is that one function point is roughly equal to 100 COBOL language statements required to program the five normalized processing activities of input, output, inquiries, logic computations, and interfaces. Extensive research establishing the reliability of the function point has been done by Software Productivity Research, Inc. (SPR), and its chairman Capers Jones. In a 1996 report of year 2000 magnitude, SPR put the function point estimate for the United States at 1,702,125,000 and the 30 most computerized countries at 7,076,560,000. Using our rule of thumb to convert to lines of code, the magnitude and obvious complexity of Y2K becomes apparent. And this indicates only the volume of known code, not home-grown, small business applications.

Complexity can be expressed not only in terms of programming languages, lines of code, and function points but in terms of the expanding number of interfaces between systems and between enterprise and its business partners and suppliers. Interdependency is the word that best describes the business and government evolution that is taking place today and for the foreseeable future. Dependency on suppliers, business partners, and external sources of information are the ways that organizations specialize and thrive. The division of labor is being optimized by information technology; but with these fine-tuned relationships come vulnerabilities. Y2K has demonstrated for all to see the special threats posed by the just-in-time world of business that has evolved over the last decade. The complexity of such relationships pose a special threat since a failure at any point of the chain results in the inability to function and fulfill commitments. In an automated business developed without standards, discipline in software development and testing, and subjected continuously to the short-term pressures of the bottom line, there exists a very fragile and brittle world of system interfaces and dependencies where "fixes" often result in cascading errors affecting all members of the chain.

From an IT industry perspective, it has been apparent since the late 1960s that the difficulties of building and maintaining large software systems had to be addressed. So from 20 years of effort, the various techniques and the discipline of software engineering were established. Software engineering is generally defined as the application of a systematic, disciplined, quantifiable approach to the development, operation, and maintenance of software.

Years later, software engineering remains an elusive goal for most organizations. Most computer code is still crafted from programming languages by skilled, and not-so-skilled, artisans using techniques that are neither repeatable nor documented. As stated elsewhere, the greatest difficulty experienced in attempting to correct the Y2K problem was in trying to figure out what many systems were doing. In the absence of documented program logic, testing materials, and other descriptive elements needed to manage software in an engineering fashion, Y2K corrective projects became chaotic exercises in puzzle solving.

And complexity can only increase as the uses of computers expand. We shall see massive changes in computing over the next 20 years; but after the Y2K experience, it should be very clear that such changes must be accompanied by techniques that assist with the management of complexity.

MANAGING IT IN THE FACE OF UNCERTAINTY

To compound the challenge of complexity, IT managers have had to construct, deliver, and maintain software systems in the face of a great deal of uncertainty. Since a successful application of IT demands considerable foresight and planning, a certain degree of certitude about business goals and objectives is desired.* If goals and objectives are clearly understood, then the application of technology will be easier than if organizational direction is in a state of confusion.

Uncertainty with regards to corporate goals and business objectives is commonly manifested in three ways.

First, business units make technical and system architectural decisions that clash with each other. This causes minimal problems if the unit is autonomous and does not have to integrate greatly for product/service reporting purposes with other business units. If too much integration is required, however, independent technological decisions and systems can create great complexity and uncertainty for those responsible for overall systems and reporting integration. If independence is allowed to any great degree, integrated and centralized systems will be under a continual cloud

---

*Some will argue that quick response and flexibility are the hallmarks of successful systems. This is true of systems that have been carefully planned and designed to be responsive and flexible.

of uncertainty as to what new directional surprise is on the horizon and how to plan for the unknown.

Second, all too often organizations suffer from what has been referred to as management by magazine. This creates an environment where usually self-proclaimed experts push for the latest and greatest technology, being unable to separate fact from marketing fiction. No systems planning model can withstand the constant interruption of the "new idea." Unless such "new ideas," in the midst of a systems development project, are subjected to some form of feasibility and risk analysis, and formally rejected or accepted, the project will never be completed. This phenomenon partially accounts for the fact that so many older legacy systems (i.e., 1960–1970 vintage) are still around. Replacement system concepts and architectures were constantly changed by the new idea and consequently were never allowed to gel and be completed.

Finally, mergers and acquisitions often are made without sufficient attention given to the technological aspects of the deal. This can have a couple of serious consequences. First, the uncertainty surrounding the complexity of integrating similar but different automated processing systems may not be reflected in the "due diligence" analysis required of the acquiring company. Therefore, risks, material risks, may not be adequately identified, considered, and reported. This could leave the acquiring company open to lawsuits and regulatory action. Second, the action of merging two IT departments because of an acquisition usually means layoffs for the acquired department. Obviously, this can result in morale problems and staff defections at a very vulnerable time for both companies.

The fast pace of the underlying technology, however, and the speed with which IT products and companies come and go pose a special challenge. In the last two decades, as the frequency of IT mergers, acquisitions, and buyouts has intensified, it has become very difficult to have much confidence that a chosen IT product or company will be around to render knowledgeable support during the anticipated life of a corporate computer system. The truth of the matter is that the acquiring company usually has a bias for its own revenue-generating products. The acquired company is likely to lose, usually in the first year, many of its key people, and so continued support of its products suffers. If a company was depending on the products and services of the acquired company, the IT manager may be in for a few surprises. This scenario is being played out on a continuous basis and can sabotage the best-planned systems.

A considerable degree of certitude in the viability, reliability, and trustworthiness of IT suppliers is also required in order to reduce the degree of uncertainty.

SUCCESSFUL SYSTEMS REQUIRE MORE THAN COMPUTERS

During the period of 1997 through 1999, all Y2K attention was turned to the computer code that needed correction. As remediation lagged it became fashionable to speak in terms of contingency plans and manual "workarounds." Thus, belatedly it was acknowledged that year 2000 was a business or government process issue and not just a computer problem.

In this same roundabout way, most systems built in the last 30 years have concentrated on computer technology first and on the human aspect second. Because of this tendency, it has been easy for the mismatches of Exhibit 1.1 to take place. Seldom have the capabilities of computers and their new technological advancements been applied after task organization and human factor issues have been designed to complement the technological element. More commonly, the new computer capability is in the forefront of the design, and the human element (i.e., employee and customer) must play catch-up. Never mind that the automated phone answering system is disliked by customers and makes their experience with a company distasteful. Never mind that "help" screens are designed and written by computer programmers and therefore confusing to the system user. Never mind that employees must scroll through endless screens to get the one that is needed for the transaction they are processing.

The irony of the Y2K problem is that in order to keep business processes flowing in the face of systems failure, the fallback is onto the human element of an overall process that was neglected from the very beginning. Once again, humans are expected to adjust to the computer—even though their needs are not accommodated in the original system's design. Exhibit 1.4 depicts the integration of technical tasks and interfaces with the social/workplace elements needed to build systems where human job-related requirements are considered part of the overall design. Use of this model allows a full analysis of the people-work component of a business process. While they are reasonably equipped to work with the technological elements of a system, most computer system developers have little or no understanding of the key elements of Exhibit 1.4—the boxes in the center and

Exhibit 1.4 Design Topics in the Sociotechnical Design of Systems

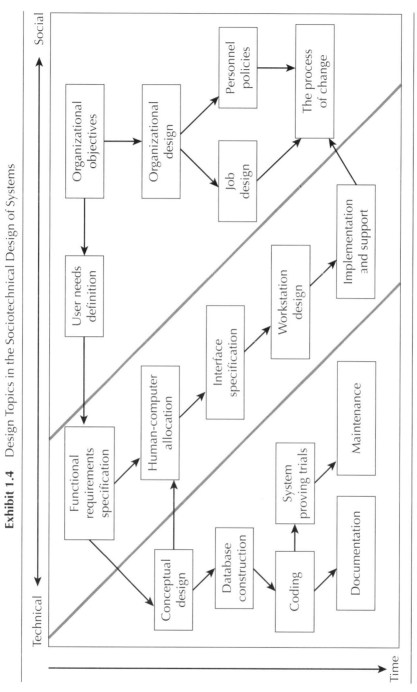

Source: Adapted from Ken Eason, *Information Technology and Organizational Change* (London: Taylor & Francis, 1998), 12, 33, 55.

to the right. With most automated systems, the majority of effort is directed to the left of the figure, often at the expense of designing the people-work component. Because of the great difficulty experienced in getting the computer components to work reliably, the human and workplace side of the system not only gets neglected but is often saddled into spending an inordinate amount of time and effort in the *care and feeding* of the error-prone computer. Is it any wonder that most systems are not considered successful by their users?

TOO MUCH—TOO SOON

No other industry has grown as fast as the computing and information technology industry. A comparison of the rate of computing advancement with the aviation industry probably would place a person on the moon during the 1930s. In fact, placing a human on the moon would not have been possible without the advancements in computing. While such rapid advancements have brought many benefits, they also have resulted in a situation where many automated systems have outstripped an organization's ability to properly support and maintain them. One of the reasons that accurate documentation has been so difficult to develop and maintain is that the pent-up demand for developing new applications generally took top priority while documentation of just-finished applications could always be completed later. Deferring the completion of documentation assures that systems running today will not be accurately represented in the systems library. Soon application software documentation is out of sync with those programs executing in day-to-day production, and even minor changes can become a major chore. This single fact has been experienced by nearly everyone attempting to resolve the Y2K date problem and accounted for many of the delays in schedule accomplishment.

Over the years, conscious and unconscious decisions to defer the critical task of documentation and the adverse impact on timely resolution of the Y2K date problem was guaranteed. Since the importance of system documentation and maintenance was never truly understood, technology advancements were able to proceed, without impedence, at an even faster pace. What resulted was an avalanche of relatively undocumented systems and products flooding the marketplace. Under the best of circumstances, such rapid growth would create a confusion factor that would be difficult to manage; but add the fact that most systems and products were not properly documented for over 20 years and you have the makings of a real crisis.

Resolution of the Y2K problem, for a business or government agency, required that system programmers and operators be able to speedily integrate the various date-processing solutions from multiple vendors into one seamless date-processing solution. Add to this a few undocumented in-house systems and it is readily understandable why few organizations were completely ready for 1 January 2000. Another readily apparent manifestation of too much too soon is the lack of qualified analysts and engineers to deal with the ever-increasing demand for systems utilizing the explosive growth of the basic technology.

Persons formally educated as systems analysts have been trained to examine the IT component parts of business systems for interrelationship problems, areas of improvement, solutions, and potential opportunities for competitive advantage. Trained analysts are tasked to disassemble existing systems into component parts that can be analyzed for operational deficiencies or improvements. Analysts can then present an array of IT proposals to include cost and schedule estimates. The type of analyst that is in such critical supply acts as a general practitioner does in the medical profession, dealing with the whole system, identifying symptoms, making a diagnosis, and calling in specialists as needed. This type of analyst also can function as architect, designing an overall business solution that accounts for all design elements seen in Exhibit 1.4, again calling in specialists as needed. Finally, this type of analyst often stays involved in a general contractor role, thus protecting the business manager's interests throughout the project.

While there is an acute shortage of the type of systems analyst just described, there is no shortage of personnel carrying the title. Today "systems analysts" include people who have specialized in any number of specific vendor products and support services. To be this specialized and remain truly expert means competence is limited to one or two languages, three or four software packages, and perhaps two vendor equipment lines.

It is entirely appropriate to refer to these individuals as system analysts, as they are experts in their particular support area of IT and as they contribute to success by ensuring the proper application of their specialty area. But for the same reason, they cannot generally function as the overall information system and architectural analyst. While specialists are indeed experts in their respective areas, they may not possess the comprehensive experience to function in the executive-level/business requirements arena. Analysts who do operate well at this level first understand how business and/or government organizations function. They understand that building a successful IT system is often more dependent on politics than on technology. For them the up-to-the-minute specifics of new technologies come second. They understand the need for disciplined project management. They have been responsible for the operations as well as the development of systems, and understand the demands of customers and performance agreements. They tend to be conservative regarding the degree of risk to which they will subject a client. They understand the principles as well as the importance of quality management, and are distressed when they see them violated. They are willing to say no to a customer. There are not enough of them to meet the need.

There are other examples of too much—too soon, but they all center on the inability of the industry as a whole to keep pace with the speed of technical developments and the inevitable problems this leads to. The only solution is to continually temper the enthusiasm for the new and wonderful with a measured degree of caution and a healthy skepticism for the much-ballyhooed short-term competitive advantage as compared to the long-term and mutually beneficial business partner relationship.

2

THE MANAGEMENT OF TECHNOLOGY PROBLEMS

It should not be surprising that there are many problems associated with the successful management of IT given the recent experience of Y2K and the fundamental misconceptions that surround the technology and its uses. The organizational, sociological, and work process adjustments required because of the use of IT requires the creation of new management models. Previous models that were based on controlling traditional "precomputer assets" do not prove sufficient for the automation-dependent enterprise. For example, precomputer management models revolved around people, money, and materials being the factors of production and the resources requiring management. Today information and time should be added to the resource list and for good reason. Computers allow the rapid access and communications of vast stores of information by decision points across the organization in order to more efficiently and effectively utilize the other resources to produce or deliver corporate products or services. It has been argued that the resources of information and time are, in fact, more important than the other resources because timely information provides to decision makers the status conditions of the other resources. Without such information presented in a timely fashion, their effective utilization could not be possible. This fact places a burden on the information to be *accurate* and to be available for access and presentation in a *timely* enough fashion to affect decisions being made and actions taken. This burden, over the years, has resulted in the need to devise *methods* and *rules* for designing and developing the systems that deliver such information. These methods and rules constitute the essential core business of information technology, not computers, chips, wire lines, and program code. And yet all too often, the methods and rules of information systems development have taken a back seat to the bit, byte, and speed of the hardware. This is understandable since hardware is tangible. It can be touched and traditional rules of accounting can be used to depreciate it. Not so the methods and rules used to build the information processing programs, databases, edit routines, presentation software, and networks for communicating information. Methods include the policies and procedures, analytic activities, systems development, process steps, and project management needed to deliver and operate a functioning automated system. Rules expressed as programmed instructions define how the system actually will perform its data processing task. Methods and rules are intellectual constructs and do not conform to the traditional models for managing more tangible items. Methods and rules, like the information products they create and give form to, are abstract and difficult to manage. Methods and rules are intellectual constructs accomplished with no clear-cut standards and with no generally accepted system of metrics used for accountability. The fundamental issues that have stymied effective management of IT begin with the lack of metrics.

FAILURE TO USE METRICS TO MANAGE IT

With management of the traditional factors of production, people, money, and materials, elaborate accounting methods have evolved around precisely defined measures for forecasting, utilization, and effectiveness. Measurements, gathered over time, serve as a "dashboard" displaying corporate activity to be monitored constantly by executive management and external audit groups for indicators of present and future corporate profitability. Dashboard information is updated continually through management reporting systems, audited for accuracy, and utilized in making budgeting, forecasting, product, marketing, operational, and many other executive and board-level decisions.

While the activities of information technology can be measured in numerous ways, the fact is that most organizations do not employ such metrics in any comprehensive fashion. Appendix A identifies the most commonly available metrics used for determining the effectiveness and efficiency of IT systems development and their operation. Without measurement, corporate management is flying blind when asked to account for how an IT asset is being utilized and whether its use falls into an acceptable range when compared to industry averages.

An examination of Appendix A will show that computers, hardware, software, communications, system development, and personnel factors are included. Upon reflection, an executive would have to ask: How has IT management been accomplished historically if such information is not known? The answer is that, generally, the use of metrics has been spotty and usually limited to operational and throughput measures associated with hardware performance. These measures of throughput, downtime, and vendor maintenance response time are linked directly to the availability of a system to its users. These uptime metrics are highly visible and difficult to ignore—although many operational managers are still surprised when a performance measure such as attempted system accesses, which has been increasing slowly, suddenly results in severe degradation in overall system response time.

The more difficult area of IT requiring the collection and use of measurement data deals with software and its development. This one area of IT management deficiency contributes more than any other to the inability to manage IT as one would other aspects of the business. In fact, this deficiency directly and indirectly contributes to many of the other problems discussed in this section.

Again, a review of Appendix A reveals that many of the recommended metrics deal with the methods and rules previously discussed.

There are metrics that measure key aspects of an organization's software and systems development methods; and there are metrics that measure the efficacy of code being programmed. Taken collectively, these metrics give insight to the quality of both the systems and the code that the IT organization is producing. These metrics essentially keep track, over time, of the quality of products being generated by the IT development staff or contractor and the staff's productivity relative to quality. Note the caveat "relative to quality." Productivity measures (i.e., lines of code generated per day) without a corresponding quality measure (i.e., debugged, tested, and fully documented) is counterproductive. It only encourages the quick generation of "buggy" code that is not maintainable and should not be put into production.

But without measures being recorded and analyzed, management cannot begin to make improvements to the methods and processes or get appropriate assistance and training for the challenged programmer. Without metrics it becomes impossible to improve on project estimates, plans, and budgets. Without metrics it becomes difficult to evaluate "progress against the plan." Without metrics an IT services company will have a very difficult time writing a bid proposal that it has confidence in. Without metrics the foundation on which effective IT management can be built does not exist. Without metrics IT decisions will continue to be made based on fear, favoritism, secret agendas, politics, and misconceptions.

LACK OF MANAGEMENT INVOLVEMENT RESULTS IN MULTIPLE RISKS

Without metrics and measurement systems it becomes very difficult to make defensible IT decisions, give work assignments, monitor programs, and evaluate performance. And yet most IT organizations do not have measurement programs in place, and often senior executives do not ask for supporting data when given estimates or projections. All too often, executive managers, because of a lack of familiarity with technology measures, make IT decisions solely based on cost and their intuitive political sense. While cost, in the abstract, is the one great normalizing metric, meaning that all other ways of measurement should be able to be reduced to cost, many aspects of IT cannot be accounted for easily in this manner. For example, the entire arena of IT-related risk management is too immature, with little or no reliable data, to be reduced to a cost factor alone. IT risk has many aspects that are only beginning to surface as system complexity grows, the number of critical applications increase, and the degree of dependencies on other systems and supplier/providers soar.

While cost/benefit studies balance costs to be incurred against anticipated benefits, the discipline of risk management attempts to balance preventive costs to be incurred against losses to be avoided or, if not avoided, at least lessened. Without risk assessments as a conscious input to IT decision makers, projects take on the unreal impression of being risk free. All corporate decisions have some degree of risk that needs to be considered. IT system decisions, with their well-documented failure rates (see Exhibit 1.2), certainly need to consider risk formally, and yet this is rarely done. With technology and implementation risks not being formally assessed, the only risk that does seem to have credence with executives is the risk of being left behind, of not capitalizing on some technological breakthrough that will change the course of history and the way business should be conducted. While these are very valid concerns, without an awareness of the accompanying risks, new technologies can be chancy and very expensive to implement, operate, and maintain in their early stages of evolution. The technology closet is full of technically attractive applications that in implementation have not delivered on their marketing promise. For example, who today remembers the name of the original technological implementation of the videotape? Likewise, who remembers the company that fielded the first working local area networks? Technological implementations and the companies promoting them come and go. They can present a definite threat to the productive operation of a business unless certain risks are recognized as being possible and are analyzed for potential adverse impact. Without this analysis, IT decisions become excessively skewed to the positive. Without a risk-tempered orientation, new technology proponents naturally will present only the positive images of progress and increased profitability—never the potential downsides. Information technologists tend to be optimistic by nature, believing that any technological challenge can be solved given enough time and money. That is the prevailing view of the culture, and it is certainly the belief of most computer people. They love a challenge. And they especially love "new" technology projects for the beneficial effect such projects have on their resume. Executive management must be cautious of this tendency to overoptimism on the part of technologists. Executive management also must be careful not to stifle technologists' expressions of caution by promoting an excessively "gung-ho" environment where anyone expressing a thoughtfully hesitant position is viewed a nonteam player. Be thankful for such viewpoints and explore the validity of the voiced concern.

To balance the influence of "rose-colored glasses" promoters, business executives need to actively encourage the risk analyses and begin by considering the following risks that are commonly associated with new technological applications:

- The proposed technology is not stable and ready for the demands of the workplace. It probably functions well in a controlled laboratory environment or it would not have been marketed—but it is not reliable under steady workload conditions. This can be true of software as well as hardware.

- The proposed technology is constructed of components that are limited and difficult to obtain. Software is written in an esoteric language, and the programmers fluent in the software are few and expensive. This can result in a situation where a company can be held hostage.
- The proposed technology is too limited in scope of functionality. It does too little to be worth the effort of implementation.
- The proposed technology is too broad in scope and provides unneeded capabilities that serve to expose an operation to accidentally triggered system downtime. Such technology also subjects a company to forced vendor upgrades having, perhaps, no benefit for the business.
- The proposed technology may not interface well with other corporate systems and contributes to an already complex situation. This generally occurs in organizations that are excessively decentralized and with no unifying common architecture or standards.
- The source of the proposed technology is not a viable business entity. It is close to bankruptcy and its employees are looking elsewhere for job security.

To deal competently with the issue of IT risk, corporations need to adopt a risk analysis philosophy and incorporate risk assessments into the thought process used during system development efforts. Integral to Exhibit 1.3 is an early analytic step known as the feasibility study. When there is a clear understanding of corporate business objectives, IT constraints, regulatory requirements, and general economic guidelines, a feasibility study, properly conducted, can serve as an effective risk analysis vehicle.

THE FEASIBILITY STUDY:
NEGLECTED TOOL OF IT MANAGEMENT

The process of bringing information technology to bear in solving a business problem or to exploit a perceived opportunity is one of selective elimination. To choose the best technology solution from among many possibilities is to perform a systematic feasibility study on each and every proposed solution.

Something is feasible if it is "capable of being managed, utilized, or dealt with successfully," according to *Webster's Third International Dictionary*. If something is feasible, it is generally considered to be reasonable and possible. The purpose of a feasibility study then is to choose a technological proposal, from among several, and an accompanying strategy for implementation that is likely to be managed, utilized, and dealt with successfully. Feasibility studies, done correctly, lead an organization to a best possible course of technical action given a clear problem or opportunity statement and a respectable level of competence of those proposing solutions. Feasibility studies can assist in selecting the best proposal for the enterprise from among many good solutions, and they also can assist in selecting the best from among multiple poorer choices. In either case, the course of action selected is one that the company can live with successfully, because all factors important to success have been considered.

These observations may seem obvious, but in fact very few comprehensive feasibility studies are ever performed. This is one of the overriding reasons for IT's poor track record when it comes to applying the technology to business problems. No one can succeed at implementing infeasible proposals. By definition, an infeasible course of action is incapable of being *managed, utilized,* or dealt with *successfully.* And every reason why a proposal is thought to be infeasible identifies for executive management an area of overall risk that may need to be monitored closely regardless of which proposal finally is selected. Knowledge of any aspect of infeasibility also should lead to modification in the proposal itself. It is an iterative process that, if *not* short-circuited, leads to doable systems and successful implementations.

TECHNICAL, OPERATIONAL, ECONOMIC: TESTS OF FEASIBILITY

There are three traditional factors of feasibility: (1) technical, (2) economic, and (3) operational. Each factor is important in its own right, but it is through their collective trade-offs that they provide a process of elimination function whereby the best possible course of action is determined. The challenge for the executive is to require that balance be maintained during the course of the study and that no one factor gain preeminence over the deliberations. Only the most senior executives can possess the strategic view and exercise the authority necessary to achieve this balance.

Usually, an IT proposal is analyzed first to review technical feasibility, then to study economic feasibility, and finally to consider operational issues. This approach, however, is likely to perpetuate the reality of Exhibit 1.2 since it is very difficult to back away from a technically sound proposal that appears to have a good economic projection just because of a few perceived operational problems. And yet, business should be concerned primarily with the operational impacts of a new technology on the workplace and the employers and on customer satisfaction. If an IT proposal passes both the technical and economic tests and yet is potentially disruptive to the workplace or damages customer relations, it cannot be considered a feasible solution. Actually, by *not* considering the negative costs associated with recovering from operational problems, processing errors, lost productivity, and customer disaffection, the economic analysis becomes dangerously incomplete in the first place and therefore misleading. It was incomplete and misleading because it was accomplished too soon and without the necessary information that would have been generated if an operational feasibility analysis had been performed first.

A more effective sequence for performing the feasibility analysis would be to conduct the technical study first, followed by the operational study, and then submit each surviving proposal to an economic comparison. Unfortunately, this sequence is seldom followed. In fact, the majority of information system decisions usually are reached on the basis of a cost study only, and few, if any, operational issues are considered from an economic perspective.

To improve the track record of IT projects, the feasibility study must be revitalized as a critical decision-making technique and completed in a comprehensive manner. The sequence in which the study is conducted is important, or else the final outcome is skewed and system decisions may become infeasible.

REQUIRE THE GENERATION OF ALTERNATIVE SOLUTIONS

For an IT systems proposal to be judged feasible, it should have been analyzed in light of the following issues and considerations.

First, technologists consider almost all technology proposals to be feasible. Given enough time and money, almost any technology solution can be made to work. The question is whether a business has the resources, time, and patience to commission what all too often turns out to be a research and development effort. If this trial-and-error route is not appealing, then the first hurdle to be cleared by a technology proposal is whether the proposal appears, on its face, to satisfy the goals of the business opportunity statement or to solve the business problem. These statements of goals and problems constitute the requirements, and it is hoped that each technical proposal represents an alternative way of satisfying the requirement.

Discussions about alternatives are important because such sessions help both the business manager and the IT analyst clarify their understanding of the requirement. In the search for alternative ways to satisfy the business requirement, the IT analyst continues to gain greater understanding of the requirement by presenting managers and/or customers with rather specific processing proposals and operational scenarios. Each proposed alternative (usually two or three) formulated from the analyst's understanding of the business need allows the business manager to determine the analyst's grasp of that need. It also allows the business manager to rethink and reaffirm his or her own understanding of the need and its importance. The IT analyst knows that the definition of requirements is not a one-time exercise; it is an iterative process that needs to culminate in a proposal statement that is clear and concise enough to be submitted to the feasibility analysis. To qualify, the proposal must at least appear to satisfy the business requirement.

TECHNICAL FEASIBILITY

Technical feasibility evaluates each proposed alternative to answer a number of important questions. Does the proposed solution employ a proven and reliable use of the technology or new and relatively untried hardware, software, and operational methods? Remember, technology is supposed to ease business processing or provide a competitive advantage that is not going to create problems. In the experience of many IT veterans, the more a technology is advertised in the commercial IT news media, the less reliable it probably is and the higher the risk in using it before it matures.

A technical proposal should be straightforward. There should be few unanswered questions about whether it will work and whether it can be supported by the IT organization or the contractor world.

If the technical proposal is to be operated and maintained by in-house employees, it must be compatible with their basic skill sets or else a training program should be included as part of the proposal. Learning a software package is one thing; learning a new architectural approach is quite another. For example, going from back-room data processing to a client/server environment is a quantum change.

If the proposal is to be supported by outsourcing or contractor assistance, there should be a stable and reasonably large workforce capable of implementing the considered solution. If the proposed solution is too unique and esoteric, the fewer the number of people who will understand it and the higher their price tag. Also, the very real threat of being held hostage by those few employees or contractors who understand a unique and nonstandard systems solution should not be underestimated.

The technical solution should not overly challenge the aptitudes and abilities of workplace employees. The purpose of the technical systems solution is to make employees more efficient and effective, not less.

Finally, does a training curriculum exist for obtaining the needed skills for systems operation and maintenance? Does this training extend beyond the technical aspects and into the employee work processes that are new or changing? If all the required training is not available in-house or from the vendor, can needed skills be obtained through the local community college or a certification program? Training issues and the ability to equip employees to use the new system productively lie at the heart of the next test of feasibility.

OPERATIONAL FEASIBILITY

Operational feasibility is the most overlooked aspect of deciding on an automated course of action "that can be managed, utilized, or dealt with successfully." Operational feasibility asks that we balance the often-overstated benefits of a new technology with the practical. How will this new technology or solution function in the corporate work environment, with employees, at their level of technical competence, and with customers? The desired application of technology enhances quality and performance of specific work activities in specific ways and is not disruptive in any way. This does not mean that things do not change; it does mean that necessary changes are identified at the time of this analysis and taken into account in identifying the most feasible solution. Changes to employee work processes, customer interfaces, and even what is expected of the customer in order to continue doing business with a company must all be considered. Each change has a cost associated with it. These costs need to be identified and quantified as far as possible. All changes have costs that can be measured in terms of time, money, and convenience or inconvenience, and these measures apply to systems maintenance personnel, workplace employees, and customers. For example, many older Americans are adapting to new electronic ways of conducting their lives, but many other millions are not and will take their business to less technically demanding competitors if pushed too fast. It is important to factor in customer reaction to a new technology solution before making final decisions. It is also wise to consider the impact on employees to preclude any unnecessary turnover. While it is understood and desired that new technologies change the ways in which business is conducted, management decides how much and how fast the company, employees, customers, and business partners can absorb such change. To help make this judgment call, the following issues should be considered.

• *Be sure to proceed with a clear understanding of the current level of customer and business partner satisfaction.* Take care not to risk losing good relations by pushing a technical solution that is unproven and has questionable customer or business partner acceptance. Let someone else test the waters and learn from their mistakes. Remember that a company usually has at least a couple years before it must begin worrying about falling behind competitors in the adoption of most technologies that end up changing the way business is conducted. Even the fast-paced rush to web-based applications has been extremely slow to show profits, and it is still not clear whether the average consumer will make web-based commerce a way of life until security and privacy problems are solved.

Regarding business partners, it is wise to adopt new technologies only after taking them fully into account by factoring in whether they will be subjected to burdensome conversion costs and other operational consequences. What appears to be good for a company may not be good for business partners. Be prepared to subsidize their transition, if their reluctance could damage implementation. It is far more expensive to replace a good customer or business partner than it is to move more slowly and deliberately to keep the current business base intact.

- *Determine the competitor's technology competence.* Don't risk market share and satisfied customers unless there is a clear advantage in doing so. Be careful not to put at risk any core business proficiencies for which the firm is known while pursuing a new technology with its unproven promise of new and better business returns. It is advisable to run *pilot projects* to learn how successful large-scale implementations can be accomplished. To move too fast is to risk neglecting the current and probably successful way of doing business. Those employees dedicated to running the current system may not feel involved. And many fear for their future. Such fears can lead to defections from the ranks with the end result being a decline in current system performance and the degree of customer satisfaction the company now possesses.

- *Factor in to the evaluation each of the changes to the current way of doing business that will be required to absorb each proposed alternative smoothly.* Referencing Exhibit 1.4, included are those changes that employees in the workplace will encounter in operating each new technical proposal while still giving excellent service to customers. Also included are changes that customers must adapt to in order to continue doing business with the company.

- *Consider employees' level of technology sophistication and their ability to adapt to the new technology solution.* Adequate training dollars should be factored into this part of the evaluation. Paul Straussman, noted IT consultant and a former assistant secretary of defense for Information Systems, U.S. Department of Defense, has estimated that overall training costs should approach $2 to $3 for each dollar spent on hardware and software. This may seem high if the technical alternative being examined is a commonly used desktop software package; but sophisticated and tailored business systems may exceed the $2 to $3 estimate when all aspects of system use, administration, and life-cycle maintenance are considered. As shall be discussed in the next section, true life-cycle system costs are for the most part greatly underestimated. One of the expenses that is generally glossed over are these initial and ongoing costs to train systems people adequately to support and maintain a system they did not build and to prepare system users to use the system successfully and to fully exploit its capabilities. Unfortunately, most new employees learn to use an automated system that supports their job performance from another employee using a technique known as on-the-job training. All too often, one employee's imperfect and incomplete knowledge and understanding of the system and its capabilities is passed on to the next person. After several iterations of this scenario, the company experiences a degradation in overall performance as a form of paralysis and Alzheimer's sets in.

• *Factor in a level of effort to administer and maintain the system over its anticipated life.* Often this critical operational reality is missing from an economic analysis, and yet it is generally accepted that as high as 70 percent of all IT budget dollars go for systems maintenance. Many will argue about what is included in maintenance, but regardless of what items are finally determined for costing purposes, this category of systems support workload must be considered an operational feasibility issue that needs examination. Remember that any aspect of a systems proposal that introduces risk to its successful implementation will also introduce risks to its operation and maintenance.

• *Determine the ease of expanding each proposed technical alternative to meet anticipated business growth demands.* Promoters often use the words "flexibility" and "ease of expansion" to market the idea that the solution can be adapted easily to changing business requirements and increased volumes. These claims need to be examined carefully based on quantitative estimates, not just vague generalities. If possible, different system workload requirements and transaction volumes should be projected for different times in the anticipated system's life. Proposed configurations to satisfy those projections then can be prepared and evaluated through research or simulations. Each proposed configuration should be examined for operational impacts and costed.

• *Evaluate the* capability *and the* desire *of the solution provider to continue support of the alternative being examined.* Obviously, these two issues are difficult to address with any certitude, but they need to be discussed openly. Determining capability and desire becomes a problem of divining the future of another company. For example, the capability of a solution provider's company to meet a firm's need today may be seriously jeopardized tomorrow following a buyout or merger. Buyouts and mergers eventually tend to destroy much of the capability of the purchased company as key people often leave or are forced out. Determining the future capabilities of a solution provider involves anticipating its business plan. Determining whether the technical solution being considered is on the solution provider's critical path for business growth is important. To buy a solution today only to discover, a year or two from now, that it must be changed because the solution provider no longer desires to support the system can lead to great unexpected inconvenience and expense. Certain IT providers are so large that no one can do anything to prevent this business reality. All the more reason to anticipate, during the operational feasibility analysis, that it will likely occur and factor such disruption in to the overall evaluation.

• *Determine the adequacy of systems documentation.* Documentation functions as the blueprints and engineering drawings of the system and are absolutely essential for systems operations, maintenance, and upgrades to be carried out smoothly. If the system is to be operated and maintained in-house, then documentation may be the most important part of the system being built or purchased. Perhaps the most effective way to judge the soundness of a systems proposal for an off-the-shelf package is through the quality of the documentation generated and assembled. The fact that an entire publishing industry has been created to explain clearly how to use the latest vendor-documented software speaks to the quality of vendor documentation. Most software and systems documentation is written by technical people for use by other technical people, not for system users who are trying to do their jobs. Failure to evaluate the reputation of the solution provider for usable documentation can undermine the most elegant technical solution.

It is important to remember to dampen enthusiasm and be a little skeptical during the operational feasibility analysis, especially since each solution's promoter will be pushing hard for his or her favored alternative. It is important to have at least one senior IT analyst stressing the livability of each alternative and playing devil's advocate while letting business line managers conclude which solution is best for operational success.

Having determined which technical alternatives are operationally feasible, attention now turns to the economic analysis.

ECONOMIC FEASIBILITY

The economic feasibility of a technical proposal should be considered last, or else the probability is high that an organization's technological direction will be determined for the wrong reason, namely, low acquisition cost, without full consideration of the many hidden operational costs and customer/business partner–borne expenses. Since the actual hardware and software components of a proposed solution are only partial means to improved business performance and/or profitability, the totality of that business process needs to be considered. These other factors associated with satisfying a business goal were examined during the operational feasibility study and the hidden costs were identified. Without full consideration of these costs, many recent economic studies have been overly influenced by the falling costs of hardware. Also, most economic analyses have not fully identified the costs associated with software and its maintenance, and so such studies are all too often drastically distorted by only a few of many important cost elements.

Good cost analysts know this and will lobby for a more complete costing picture, but they are usually thwarted by several things.

First, since IT performance, development, and operational metrics are not commonly kept, there are no clearly identified IT costs except for hardware and the numbers of employees supporting or working with the system. All that is known in most organizations is that purchased or leased hardware costs so much, communication expenses are such and so, and the total payroll of the system people is X. And that payroll keeps rising. Without internal IT metrics to measure what systems people are doing and how well they are doing it, intelligent costing and project management is difficult.

Second, the shortcomings of the costing picture generally are overwhelmed by the great promise of future benefits and revenues. The theoretical promise of riches because of the impact of a breakthrough technology on any business has great appeal. It is often justified as an investment in the future and the need to beat competitors to the punch.

Third, even if measurement data were kept, it would take time to establish a company profile of performance and determine the baselines needed for costing future technology initiatives.

If complete costing data is so important to performing a reliable economic analysis, and most companies do not have it, what is actually happening during this phase of the feasibility analysis and what are the implications?

BALANCING COSTS AND BENEFITS

Exhibit 2.1 depicts many cost items that should be considered in a comprehensive economic analysis. These are arranged in terms of one-time acquisition/procurement/recruitment/construction costs, and ongoing operational and upgrade costs. To get an accurate picture of the cost aspects of a proposal, the elements of Exhibit 2.1 should be estimated for each alternative proposal and entered on the cost side of the economic analysis equation.

Of course, any decision to expend dollars on technology is usually justified to corporate financial managers through the identification of increased revenues, reduced costs, or the benefits that accrue from new and better services designed to retain or capture customers. A true picture of benefits to be realized from choosing one technical proposal over another can only be estimated after an evaluation of impact on the overall business process being modified by the proposal. Thus, the following questions must be asked in order to cut through the theoretical promises of vague riches. Will the benefits from a technically and operationally feasible solution come through:

- Reduced overhead or production costs? How will the benefits be measured?
- Increased productivity and/or increased revenue? How will it be measured?
- Improved customer service? How will it be measured?
- New business products and services through better use of information?
- Increased sales and expanded customer base through better use of market data?

Over the last three decades, the justifications that have usually been used include reduced overhead and production costs coupled with increased productivity. Sometimes these are two sides of the same coin, but usually they are presented as if they were two separate sets of benefits. In retailing it is true that automation has reduced the overhead costs of keeping inventories by designing just-in-time ordering and delivery systems. Likewise, in manufacturing, inventory and production costs have been reduced by im-

Exhibit 2.1   Items to Consider in Cost Analysis

	Acquisition costs	Operating costs	Upgrade costs
Hardware equipment	Equipment purchase or lease and installation	Maintenance/warranty Annual lease/rental security	Hardware replacement or upgrades
Software	Software One-time license Initial charges	Annual licensing Maintenance fees Warranty security	Software replacement or upgrades
Personnel	Recruiting Training and education Planning, design, and selection Hardware and software programming Testing	Routine monitoring and operations Problem determination and correction User liaison and administration Programming maintenance	User changes Software changes and upgrades Training and education Programming Contract programming
Communications	Initial hardware and hookup	Monthly charges Hookup Security Tariffs	Additional lines and equipment
Facilities	Facilities development Wiring Security Plumbing	Floor space Power Air conditioning Security	Incremental wiring Incremental space Increased security

proved and quicker methods. But these justifications are beginning to come into question as reductions in overhead continue to result in downsizing of the administrative support workforce and the elimination of middle management. Some observers as eminent as Peter Drucker have wondered at the long-term wisdom of continuing to eliminate middle management and senior-level support personnel on the assumption that IT systems will not only pick up the slack when people are let go but also will significantly improve the productivity of those remaining. In his book *Managing for the Future,* Drucker questioned whether any actual productivity improvements had been experienced in the white-collar arena after some 20 years of automating administrative and management work functions. One of the more serious difficulties appears to be that corporations and government agencies, through excessive reductions in midlevel employees and managers, are losing their collective corporate memory. Now, some will undoubtedly argue that in this fast-moving technological age, corporate memories tend to tie employees to the old ways of doing business. What is needed, it is argued, are employees who are continuously reevaluating and reinventing business processes and the very business itself. At the same time, it must be recognized that while all this exciting and innovative reengineering and reinventing is going on, the business, like it or not, is probably going to remain largely dependent on legacy systems developed many years ago. In some cases these systems are well into their second or third decade of use. The wrong personnel reductions or too many reductions, made in the name of short-term cost savings, can threaten the viability of these systems and the business itself.

This is one of the grim lessons learned from the recent Y2K experience. For years, *personnel reductions were made before* a new-generation replacement system was fully fielded, and then *more personnel reductions* were made before yet a newer replacement system for the first replacement system was fully fielded. To justify each replacement system, people, and ignorantly the functions they performed, were eliminated or laid off. The problem is that with systems that were never fully implemented the new way of doing business was never stabilized before those employees who were continuing to operate the old system—and therefore the company—were let go. Two or three iterations of this scenario and corporations, when faced with the Y2K problem, awoke to the fact that few people understood the old systems, despite the company being dependent on those systems to a distressing degree.

Oftentimes, what also has occurred is that the basic misunderstanding between what people do well and what computers are supposed to do surfaces, and a company is left not only with fewer and fewer people but with systems that are operationally incongruent and difficult to administer on a daily basis.

This is why the areas of technical and operational feasibility were examined first. Care must be taken to conduct the economic analysis only on alternatives that will satisfy the opportunity and/or problem statement with as little disruption as possible. Without this assurance, a seemingly favorable economic analysis, based primarily on an employee and cost reduction strategy, could condemn the business to a situation where the anticipated cost reductions and benefits are overwhelmed by the unanticipated costs associated with making the system work with too few and inexperienced people. Here the term "favorable" is used in the sense that most economic analyses cannot adequately take into account the intangible factors that can negatively affect the workforce or customers. These unanticipated negative factors provide additional justification for considering a slower pace in embracing too new a technology. Consider letting others explore this technology first and benefit from observation.

To get a truer picture of those cost items that can be identified and quantified, refer again to Exhibit 2.1. Be sure that each item of potential cost is addressed and that all items for which there are no estimates are explained as to why they do not apply to the alternative under analysis. Typically, cost item estimates associated with most technology proposals cover only a small number of the items reflected in the exhibit. Often, a proposal's promoter supplies only hardware and software estimates and usually for acquisition only, thus reflecting the upper portion of the exhibit. In so doing, the promoter fails to acknowledge as much as two thirds of the system's lifetime cost. This tendency to present partial cost projections may be one reason why IT managers have credibility problems with other executives. But an equally serious issue is why those executives have accepted this incomplete picture and allowed projects to proceed anyway. The reasons for submitting incomplete cost projects vary from ignorance, to salesmanship, to the excuse "We'll worry about that later when we know more about the project!"

It becomes apparent that benefits, which offset the costs seen in Exhibit 2.1, are going to have to be sizable. For an IT effort to be successful, it must be funded and justified by enough offsetting benefits to allow it to survive the time needed for disciplined development and for an operational life of several years. This means that projected benefits over the life of the system must more than cover all of the pertinent costs in the exhibit. This is a difficult determination to make and therefore is rarely done. But such a calculation is critical to the chances for project success. A weak benefits analysis contributes to unrealistic expectations for the project and subjects the development effort to *constant pressure* to show something soon for the money. On the other hand, IT projects that are well justified by actual business process improvements and good comprehensive costing tend to have realistic benefit projections and enjoy the patience of users, management, and customers as disciplined development and implementation progresses.

While the economic analysis for most system proposals have tended to concentrate on cost reduction and productivity improvements, increasingly there are those people who seek their justification through increased or improved customer service. In view of the costs associated with a system's development, implementation, and maintenance, this benefit rationale can be difficult to state unless a great deal of information exists concerning customer behavior and their satisfaction or dissatisfaction with the current level of service. Again, this shows the importance of measurement and metrics.

If a company actively embraced the quality improvement movement of the 1980s and has been patiently implementing its principles, people know the business processes, warts and all, and the customers' degree of satisfaction with those processes. With such information an attempt can be made to justify each technical proposal based on some expression of increased service or improved quality of service. Unless a corporation is large enough, however, to run pilot projects for the purpose of gathering customer reaction data, customer service improvement justifications are generally too "soft" to withstand the universal tendency of financial managers not to spend money. In such cases, customer service improvement proposals begin to look to elements of traditional cost-reduction strategies to bolster the benefits picture and then run the risk of having employee and cost-reduction measures negate the proposal's original customer-focused benefits. For example, by using yet further staff reductions as a partial justification to keep a customer service initiative alive, a company actually may make customer service worse because the remaining employees are stretched too far to give proper service regardless of the technological improvement the new system offers. Training in customer relations and how to smile in the face of adversity cannot compensate for a system that is down, and when reservations or luggage is lost.

Referring to the list on page 32, the remaining two arguments for justifying technological proposals are relatively new and are based on working more intelligently. As justifications they are "future" based and contend that the company will be able to create new products and services while increasing sales and expanding the customer base through better use of information. These justifications are used with proposals that include the technologies of data warehousing and the use of analytic tools and modeling. Such justifications have great appeal and will be supported by numerous advocates within the company. The problem is that the benefits set forth in these justifications must be taken largely on faith, while the proposals themselves may be quite expensive. There are no guarantees that, by building these systems, breakthrough insights about customers or revolutionary products and services will be forthcoming. Much is dependent on the quality of the information stores to be analyzed and the experience of analysts in using such systems. Technical proposals that look to these justifications are not likely to be unduly judged by the expectations of also delivering reduced costs or increased productivity. Nevertheless, they are susceptible to the impatience of those who expect quick returns on their investment.

WHAT ABOUT RETURN ON INVESTMENT?

For IT, the concept of return on investment (ROI) needs to be understood within the context of the full feasibility study. Traditionally as noted, most IT expenditures have been based on cost reductions claimed to be brought about through the use of technology. But more recently an ROI has been sought from technology investments that purport to contribute strategically to the business by creating new products, discovering new customers, decreasing time to market, or increasing the company's revenue base. Of the system justifications listed earlier, the two that best support an ROI study are the final two that deal with working smarter through better analysis of data and information.

The ROI is a more appropriate method for expressing the benefits of one technology proposal over another when improved knowledge is the business goal. But to do this effectively, IT and business unit managers must work closely to identify the key metrics concerning *information value* before the system is designed and constructed. These metrics need to focus on non–cost-reduction measurements that can be used to specify the design of the system and to monitor the growth and market share increases resulting from uses of the system. If the ROI metric is not well defined (i.e., if it does not specify how long-term success will be measured), the economic analysis may be forced to revert to a cost-reduction strategy; once again, this subjects development to the pressures of a quick payback. By focusing on top-line, value-added, future improvements, brought about through better data analysis, a technical proposal may be easier to justify as long as the future that is envisioned is realistic. Do not generally look to the IT manager to develop valuation metrics for increased knowledge. Only the business units responsible for production, revenue growth, and market share can determine the value of systems providing such information. Peter Drucker in his latest book, *Management Challenges for the 21st Century,* contends that new and valuable information is beginning to be created not by the computer directly but through new accounting concepts such as economic-chain accounting and activity-based accounting. These techniques provide the analysis of value while the supporting computer supplies the necessary speed to conduct the analysis in a time frame that adds to the data's value. Such proposals are excellent candidates for an ROI study as long as the task of developing non–cost-reduction metrics for measuring eventual knowledge value improvements has been addressed.

REVISITING OPERATIONAL FEASIBILITY

As has been seen, conducting a feasibility study actually forces a process of elimination between competing technical proposals. The study usually results in a refining and merging of original alternative proposals into a hybrid solution with the best aspects of each alternative present. As a result, the final technical proposal may have been modified substantially from the first time it was subjected to the operational feasibility analysis. Now would be a good time to revisit the operational study and evaluate any new issues surrounding the final choice of solutions. Once again, the purpose of the operational feasibility analysis is to determine whether the selected, or hybrid, technical proposal can be managed, designed, developed, implemented, operated, and maintained successfully in the company's environment, with available support vendors, employees, and customers. Unless blending-edge risk is what is desired, this final reevaluation of what is realistic and practical should render a go-ahead decision for a manageable technical solution.

OTHER STUDIES NEEDED FOR SUCCESSFUL SYSTEMS

Closely related to the questions of feasibility are three additional areas of analysis that often are treated separately. With some corporations and within certain government agencies these topic areas require separate documentation showing that they have been addressed. The three areas are: (1) performance management, (2) computer security and internal controls, and (3) efficiency and customer service analysis.

Performance Management

Performance problems begin to surface when work tasks are done too slowly to satisfy the business processing requirement. Opportunities to improve performance often can be achieved by upgrading existing technology without changing the nature of the work task. The process simply is performed faster. Performance of IT systems usually is measured by throughput and response time. Throughput is the amount of work being accomplished in a given time period. Response time is the time delay between the entry of a transaction into the system and the system's response to the transaction. Technological improvements such as a faster processor, more memory, or increases in communication line capacity should be evaluated periodically and upgrades made that improve operating efficiency. Care must be taken, however, to ensure that speedups actually improve overall employee job performance. As long as the fundamental business task is not adversely impacted, such improvements should be encouraged. If a throughput or response time improvement begins to affect employee job performance or worker morale adversely, then aspects of the original feasibility study need to be revisited. Care must be taken not to end up with a workplace resembling Lucy and Ethel in the famous chocolate candy–wrapping assembly-line scene from the *I Love Lucy* show. While throughput and response time improvements often are thought of as merely technical issues, they need to be considered separately and together for their effect on the workplace environment.

Computer Security and Business Process Integrity

Many organizations, because of the sensitive or financial nature of their business, are especially threatened by breaches of computer security that compromise the integrity of the business process. Computer and information security as they relate to business integrity are complex topics that cover a multitude of situations found in most computing and computer-intensive business environments. In recent years the government has cautioned that business and government systems are highly vulnerable to unauthorized access and manipulation of processes and data and that the threat to our society is high because of our great dependence on computers and on their continuous and error-free operation.

Computer security and business process integrity are concerned with the creation and maintenance of a secured operating environment where the

Exhibit 2.2   Elements of Technical
Computer Security

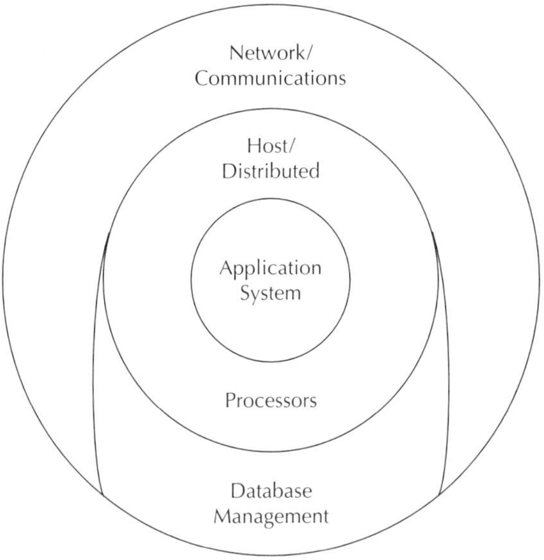

Source: Arthur Hutt, Seymour Bosworth, and Douglas Hoyt, *Computer Security Handbook,* 3d ed. (New York: John Wiley & Sons, 1995). Reprinted by permission of John Wiley & Sons, Inc.

Exhibit 2.3   Operational and Quality Specifications

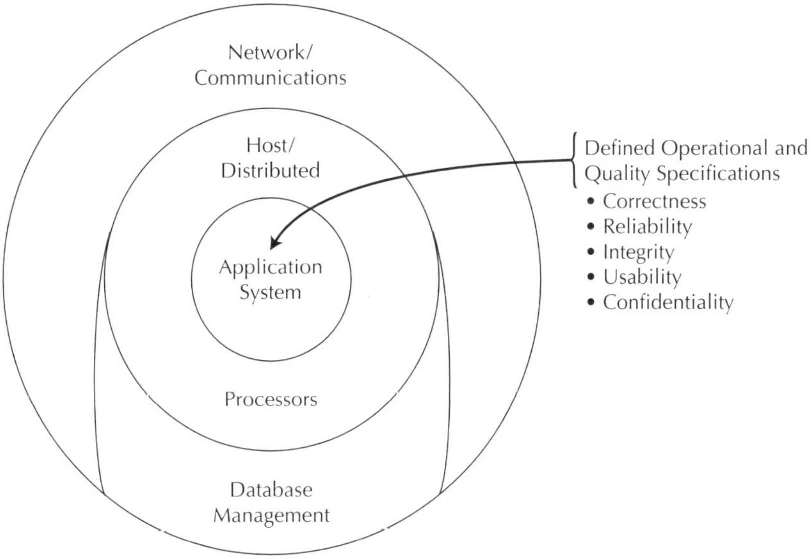

Source: Arthur Hutt, Seymour Bosworth, and Douglas Hoyt, *Computer Security Handbook*, 3d ed. (New York: John Wiley & Sons, 1995). Reprinted by permission of John Wiley & Sons, Inc.

integrity of business activities and sensitive data are guaranteed. Exhibit 2.2 depicts a business application system and its relationship to numerous technical-level support systems. From an executive perspective, a business application system can be seen as the sum of hardware, software, databases, communications, and other technologies working together to produce a desired business output. The application system is centered within the other technical systems since it is dependent on their utility and will rely on their integrity features to create a secured operating environment where the application, with its output products and services, can be considered reliable and can be trusted by the user or customer. The application system carries out a business function and executes the programmed logic of a design that best performs that function in a specified manner. The application system, then, is constructed to perform the business function according to the defined set of specifications. These specifications describe the operational and quality characteristics of the application and the parameters within which it will be trusted for use. Exhibit 2.3 shows that application systems

Exhibit 2.4   Definitions of Operational and Quality Specifications

---

Correctness: The degree to which system outputs satisfy the accuracy requirements of the business activity being supported.

Reliability: The degree to which the system is available and meets the business requirement for operational "up" time.

Integrity: A measure of completeness and soundness of design and construction. A system that has integrity can be trusted by the user.

Usability: A measure of being "fit for use" by a representative employee in the actual workplace.

Confidentiality: A measure of privacy or secrecy that is required by nature of the information involved or the sensitivity of the business process.

---

need to be described in terms of operational and quality characteristics that are specified to a degree of precision necessary to allow for accurate and productive computer program development. Without this degree of specificity, no manager, programmer, or user knows the necessary and desired parameters within which the finished software application must execute the business function. Exhibit 2.4 defines each operational and quality characteristic. No matter how the characteristics are defined, they must be specified in measurable terms or else there is no way to determine whether the finished software system can be trusted for use.

For example, it is one thing to state that the design goal of an application system is to "pay the suppliers" and quite a different thing to specify paying suppliers the accurate amount on the proper day of the month and according to the specific accounting rules of the company. Without this degree of precision, stated as a set of specifications, the computer programmer must, and will, make something up. Without this degree of precision, the system cannot be audited and probably does not satisfy the accounting rules required for business record keeping.

But even assuming clear specification of operational and quality characteristics, how can system integrity be maintained after it is programmed? How can the system be protected against breaches of security, confidentiality, and privacy? How can unauthorized and fraudulent manipulation of corporate data be prevented? How can industrial espionage be guarded against? How can computing assets be protected against physical attack that can deny services to authorized system users? How can accidental mistakes that can compromise business system integrity or bring the com-

Exhibit 2.5 Security and Internal Controls

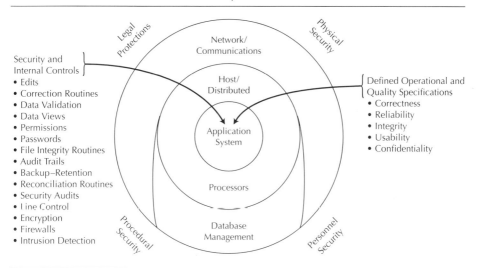

Source: Arthur Hutt, Seymour Bosworth, and Douglas Hoyt, *Computer Security Handbook,* 3d ed. (New York: John Wiley & Sons, 1995). Reprinted by permission of John Wiley & Sons, Inc.

puter down be protected against? The answer to all these questions lies in the judicious application of security and internal controls to the application system, and technical, physical, procedural, and personnel controls applied to the operating environment within which the application is run. All of these various controls are utilized within a legal framework prescribed by business rules consistent with prevailing laws and regulations.

Exhibit 2.5 depicts the categories of security and integrity controls to be applied to the systems requiring protection. Exhibit 2.6 defines common security and internal controls that need to be applied to most sensitive government and business systems if processing and information security and integrity are to be assured.

But knowledge of security and internal control techniques is only a small part of the security and integrity equation. Control techniques over computer applications have existed since the earliest days of computing. The difficult part of the security and integrity equation is knowing what needs protection and how to determine the adequacy of a technique in any given processing situation. Determining how to secure an automated system and its associated business process requires the completion of a com-

Exhibit 2.6 Security and Internal Control Definitions

Edits: Edits are defined checks and controls that ensure accuracy of input data. The sufficiency of edits and their use during the business process is based on the stringency of the quality attribute metrics. The more severe the metric, the more important the edits.

Correction Routines: Software and/or manual routines invoked to correct errors and omissions discovered by an edit.

Data Validation: Software and/or manual routines to check the accuracy and appropriateness of data before entry to a system or database.

Data Views: Subset access to a total data collection based on a predetermined need of an employee or class of employees for the data in performance of their duties.

Permissions: Actions that a user is permitted to take once access has been granted to a store of data. These permissions may be to READ, WRITE, APPEND, DELETE, EXECUTE, or any combination based on job requirements.

Passwords for Access: Access to systems, data, and the granting of permitted actions is based on recognition by the security software of a unique identification code. Passwords must be kept secure.

File Integrity Routines: Software housekeeping routines for maintaining the trustworthiness of data in a database. The more severe the accuracy requirements, the more stringent these routines and the more often they should be run.

Audit Trails: Recording of three types of processing activities: (1) logs to aid in the reconstruction of transactions; (2) logs to meet the requirements of the audit staff; and (3) logs recording security accesses, activities, and suspected violations.

Backup and Retention: Policies and procedures for ensuring the ability to reconstruct files, software, and business transactions in the event of a processing interruption or to meet a legal requirement.

Reconciliation Routines: Procedures to bring about a settlement or adjustment between differing information sources, databases, or reports.

Audit/Security Reports: Suspected violation or incident reports generated for the purpose of adjusting controls and managing system resources.

Line Control: Physical location and/or placement of controls on communication lines to prevent unauthorized access to the line.

Encryption: Encryption is a means of maintaining secure data in an insecure environment.

Firewalls: A control technique to limit access to system resources, usually a combination of hardware and software.

Intrusion Detection: Software which can detect unauthorized access and provide forensic data.

puter security and business process integrity risk analysis. Many excellent books have been written on this topic, and the need to conduct risk assessment studies of automated systems and their operational environments is not new. What would be new, and is indeed becoming an imperative for the future, is the ability to conduct such assessments with the degree of executive involvement needed to ensure their success. The same degree of involvement that resulted in a successful Y2K transition.

As with other topics in this book, the involvement of executive and senior business managers will determine the difference between success and failure of computer security and business integrity initiatives. This is because only top management can provide the overall business perspective to make the required trade-off decisions to accept or reject risk. For example, one of the reasons why computer hacking and computer fraud are perennially in the news is because most compromised systems have been poorly protected, or the organization moved into a new technology, such as e-commerce, before adequate protective techniques had been developed, implemented, and proven in the workplace. Both situations speak of how the organization did not deal successfully with the trade-offs between security controls and the open systems environments desired to promote business.

Controlling access to sensitive business information and confidential private data requires that certain impediments to easy access be developed, implemented, and maintained. Preventing or minimizing fraudulent business transactions also requires the insertion of checks and controls on incoming data and internal processes and perhaps independent confirmation (i.e., off-line) before transactions are considered valid. All too often, controlling access and taking steps to reduce fraudulent business activity are seen as slowing down business and presenting barriers to customers—besides, business losses can be written off. What cannot be written off are customers or business partners who experience loss due to breaches in security and who stop conducting business with a company.

The completion of a computer security and business process integrity *risk analysis* is a cornerstone analysis for any new system proposal, enhancement, or programming fix to an old system. The trade-offs are cost vs. loss in nature as opposed to the more traditional cost-benefit viewpoint of the economic feasibility and ROI study. There is a cost of doing IT business, and security and internal controls are part of that cost.

Efficiency and Customer Service Analysis

The last of the studies required to determine a feasible course of action for an IT initiative deals with proposals to improve operating efficiencies and customer service. Here also there are special considerations that should be taken into account.

It is often possible to confuse an efficiency and/or customer service evaluation with the economic analysis of the feasibility study. But such confusion should not exist. While an economic feasibility analysis is concerned with the resources necessary to achieve a certain reduction in operating costs, increases in productivity, or a favorable ROI, an efficiency and customer service analysis is concerned with the use of current system resources with a minimum of waste. Efficiency is closely related to the concept of cost of quality. Those familiar with the quality management initiatives of their corporation will recognize that cost-of-quality measurements provide the foundation for many business process improvements—the fine-tuning—of work processes to be more effective and efficient. Automation often provides these efficiencies. Systems destined to provide quality information or services and products are designed and developed according to quality management principles. A well-designed information system anticipates a wide range of potential errors that could occur during any step of processing and will seek to detect and require the reconciliation of these errors early in the process, where the cost to correct them is lowest. This type of efficiency, brought about through improvements to the existing business process, is often a key ingredient to obtaining or exceeding the projected benefits of the original system.

An incremental approach to improving system efficiencies is much less risky than the introduction of a whole new technology to the business process. Improvements around the edges can be substantial and do not subject the business to the risks of revolutionary change. The economics of this approach require the establishment and maintenance of cost of quality metrics, which also are needed for quality management purposes, as shall be discussed later.

The customer service analysis is performed to improve services to internal system users, to external customers, or both. The performance of a service analysis requires that an identified and measurable set of service objectives exists. The objectives that are commonly established deal with improved accuracy, increased reliability, improved ease of use, and enhanced throughput or response time.

For service analysis improvements to be successful, customers and/or users must support and agree with the service objectives and methods of measurement. This is because service improvements must take into account the nontechnical workplace aspects of the system's environment. To bring about the desired results, supporting social and organizational elements must be considered and incorporated into the implementation of the service enhancement.

It is important that both efficiency and service improvement expectations be realistic and considered feasible in every other way. Such improvements to operational business systems should be based on actual measurement and analysis and not rest on the vague promises of marketing materials. Finally, without sufficient reflection, the apparent solution to one problem may become a problem unto itself. The original questions of the feasibility study should never be far from the assessors' minds.

3

REALITIES AND CONDITIONS THAT HAVE INFLUENCED SYSTEM MANAGEMENT STRATEGIES

Associated with any information technology proposal are stated and implied expectations and assumptions concerning project development and implementation. One of the purposes of the feasibility analysis is to surface and test these assumptions. But not all issues of importance will be evaluated during the early phases of a project. Additionally, certain expectations and assumptions need careful monitoring throughout the life of the project. They need to be reviewed periodically for continued validity, from the early phases of initial project planning through to system testing, development, and business operations.

Some of these expectations and assumptions will greatly influence a project's development and implementation strategy. Some may subject the company to hidden risks that can overshadow the originally perceived gain from the system. Several of these expectations and assumptions, if not understood, can submit the organization to real dangers.

TECHNOLOGY: A SILVER BULLET FOR ALL OCCASIONS

Although somewhat tempered by the recent Y2K experience, the belief that technology is a silver bullet runs to the very heart of our technological society. In the face of all implementation challenges, we *believe!* We believe that any technology is worth the effort to develop and implement. In the abstract, and over time, this may be true. But executives are not presiding over the abstract—they oversee the reality of today's corporation. They must be pragmatic. The tests of feasibility, if performed with any degree of diligence, will support that pragmatism. The trouble with the silver-bullet mentality is that it sees technology and technological products in a mystical light, and this in a sense *gives permission not to plan and manage the technology rigorously enough.* After all, today's problem, whatever its cause or nature, will be solved by tomorrow's "breakthrough" technology or product. Someone will figure out a solution. The marketplace will rise to the occasion. The next software release will hold the answer. If thought to be true, each of these statements helps to relieve the "believer" from having to take action to control and manage the environment. Outside of the research laboratory, the silver-bullet mentality reflects a lazy approach to technology management and sets the believer up for the skilled marketeer who prefers management by magazine.

TECHNOLOGY MANAGEMENT BY MAGAZINE

"Management by magazine" is the phenomenon where technology decisions are overly influenced by the announcements of new technology products in IT and/or vertical market business journals followed by pronouncements of great benefits resulting in breathtaking profits. Because of the mystical way in which technology sometimes is viewed, decisions to embrace a hyped product often are made without a full feasibility analysis and with little regard for risk.

Just for today, I ask the reader to consciously evaluate what the preponderance of published technology articles pertaining to their business are saying. Exclude from this review IT advertisements because they are obviously marketing pieces. They have companies overcoming the "dark side of the force" by buying their product or by employing them as consultants. Interesting and exciting, yes, but hardly the materials upon which corporate IT decisions should be based.

The articles for evaluation generally are presented as the subjective account of a fellow business manager singing the praises of a new IT product or business processing technique using new IT products. In the article, difficulties encountered are seldom mentioned and the overall impression is one of great satisfaction with the product or new processing approach.

The "hidden message," the reason for which the article was written, especially if secretly commissioned by a product vendor, is that current business processes and uses of IT are threatened by this new, better, and highly successful way of doing business.

Articles of this type are written mostly to promote corporate or self-interest and to generate sales for a fledgling idea and product in an early stage of evolution. Only after many months will articles begin to appear that critique the product or new processing approach. In most cases the trigger for a follow-up article are rumors of trouble.

There is a reason that influential business executives are seldom shown the wiring closet, the back of a personal computer, or the rat's nest of cables and wires under the raised floor—they may perceive complexity and risk, not simplicity and profit. Complexity and risk may promote caution and analysis while simplicity and profit promote sales and higher revenues for the vendor.

But the real threat posed by management by magazine is that new ideas and products are legion and there is great risk to working automated business systems if they are tinkered with too frequently. There is even greater risk to a new systems development if it must accommodate endless changes and new technical ideas brought about from what people read in magazines.

The feasibility study with its risk screening process should, of course, be responsive to new ideas and suggested changes, so that it cannot be circumvented and ignored.

DOWNSIZING AND THE LOSS OF CORPORATE MEMORY

The major expectations associated with downsizing and the cost reductions and cost avoidance resulting from reductions in workforce or layoffs still are high in many industries. Whenever an increase in profitability is required or desired, the easiest way seems to be through cost-reduction strategies, and the most likely area for reductions still seems to be in personnel. After a decade of steady downsizing, though, and the risk of corporate memory loss is beginning to loom as a very real threat, especially in areas where IT has replaced more manual and labor-intensive ways of conducting the business. The truth of this reality is currently being felt by many companies as they work to recover from Y2K problems and outages. During 1999, when governments and companies were beginning their year

2000 contingency plans, it was often stated that previously automated workloads would, in a crisis, be accomplished manually. There seemed to be some appreciation for the general slowdown in business processing that might result from having to invoke the manual processing contingency, but the inability to execute at all was never or rarely questioned. What is now being realized is that some automated business processes that have evolved over the last two decades have no manual processing predecessor system to fall back to. Second, it is apparent now that organizations that failed to demand that IT systems be strictly documented are paying a heavy price as they try to figure out how business is conducted.

Too much downsizing accompanied by too great a dependence on automated systems coupled with insufficiently documented systems and an ever-mobile employee population can lead to the total inability to carry out business functions manually for an extended period of time. To make matters worse, downsizing is finding its way into the IT department itself where employee layoffs not only threaten the ability to maintain the "essential" automated system but can result in morale problems, where employees are spending much more time looking for their next job, just in case, than attending to their duties. Remember, today an IT employee can launch a secret and comprehensive job search through the Internet and never leave his or her cubicle.

One of the most amazing episodes observed during the countdown to Y2K was the announcement on the cover of *Computerworld* that a major bank, having just acquired another bank, was going to lay off most of the acquired bank's IT staff. The announcement proudly portrayed this action as a hard-nosed business decision to eliminate redundant staff and save money. One can only imagine the degree of dedication for fixing the bank's Y2K date problem that was exhibited by the staff of the acquired bank from that day forward.

Downsizing at its worst announced at the worst possible time.

EMPLOYEES AND THEIR SENSE OF LOYALTY

Whatever happened to employee loyalty? Whatever happened to that sense of individual responsibility that made a corporation great? If it is still present, be thankful. If not, look to automation and downsizing first and to employee moral qualities second.

For many reasons, employees do not feel the same sense of loyalty to their employers as previous generations, and this fact must be factored into future systems management strategies.

This reality poses special risks to systems under development and requiring long-term maintenance support. It also poses special risks because there is a scarcity of qualified IT people in the workplace and they are easily employable, generally at a moment's notice. People in IT actually can live according to the Johnny Paycheck lyric, "Take this job and shove it, I ain't working here no more."

The sociological and psychological factors closely related to the lost sense of loyalty and responsibility shall be discussed later. Suffice it for now to say that these realities must be accepted, mitigated where possible, and planned around.

System management strategies must proceed on these assumptions and allow no one individual to become so essential to a project or process as to put the company at risk. While interpersonal skills and certain management styles can help ease the risk posed by the essential person, other techniques must be employed to permit the project or the company to carry on should any individual walk out the door. These techniques include division of responsibilities, cross-training, double teaming, and demanding that all work products be thoroughly documented in an understandable manner. Without these measures being taken, a company is leaving itself in a vulnerable state and can be held hostage by any essential person.

ACCOUNTABILITY: A LACK OF CONSEQUENCES AND MEANINGFUL WARRANTIES

In a business world that has become highly integrated through the use of IT, everyone is somehow, and to some degree, dependent on the successful IT processing of the "other guy." This is the overriding lesson being learned from the Y2K experience. Put into the popular terms of the quality movement: Everyone is someone's customer, and everyone is someone's supplier. After Y2K we finally understand the source of Edward Deming's wisdom. As a world-acclaimed quality management expert, he fully appreciated the linkage between customer and supplier and the fact that, in a world of interdependencies, quality is not something that is just a good idea—it becomes essential, a matter of the viability of joint interests and cooperative business arrangements. Businesses owe quality and accountability to each other and their customers. This is the way a technologically integrated world should function, not from a position of caveat emptor. This is the way business, and especially the IT business, must operate in the next century for all to prosper.

Unfortunately, a sensitivity for the interests of customers historically has not been a high priority in the packaged software arena. With just about every other industry, buyers have ways to address the replacement or repair of faulty products. Not so with packaged software. With other industries, customers now hold their manufacturers accountable for quality and safety, and these requirements are supported by the contracting and legal systems. Not so the world of packaged software.

From the moment packaged software is installed or unwrapped, the vendor has disclaimed any reasonable expectation on the part of the buyer for a meaningful warranty. The vendor generally agrees only that ". . . software will substantially conform to the documentation." The vendor further makes ". . . no warranty or representation, either express or implied, with respect to the software, documentation, quality, performance, usability, condition, compatibility, security, accuracy, merchantability, or fitness for a particular purpose." This statement is followed by ". . . customer waives any claims even if the vendor has been advised of the possibility of dangers."

These statements mean that by proceeding to install software, the buyer/customer/user has absolved the software vendor of any responsibility for defects that may cause, for example, a security breach into sensitive files or the mistaken command that destroys a hard drive. The most a software package vendor will agree to is ". . . that the software vendor will only have to cover either the purchase price paid or the costs of repairs to the software, but only if such repairs are available," but even this warranty is disallowed in the case of the customer's "misapplication" of the software during use. And misapplication is a distinct possibility when the software must only *substantially* conform to the documentation and when its quality and usability are not good enough for the vendor to warrant.

Such warranties and remedies are meaningless and worthless. Much of the business world will shortly be engaged in a protracted legal battle to extract some degree of compensation for the damages caused by the Y2K *defect.* Much will be decisively decided if the courts accept the descriptive word "defect" as opposed to "bug." "Bugs" have become somehow acceptable to the buying public, because "bugs" are viewed as generally unforeseen and somehow akin to acts of God. As such, bugs are seen as an undesirable but necessary cost of doing business—a cost for which the software vendor accepts no responsibility.

A defect, on the other hand, implies something wrong with the process used during the building of the software production in which the defect was found. A defect is a *flaw* caused by programmers during the act of creating software. It is not an act of God. But, one might say, mistakes happen; since programmers are human and programming is a human endeavor, defects are bound to creep into the complex act of building software. Yes, mistakes happen, but mistakes can be prevented and discovered and corrected before software is delivered to customers. Why aren't they? The truth of the matter is that software is rushed to customers after incomplete inspection and testing with a disregard for the problems a defect may cause the buyer, hence the disclaimer language in the warranty. Notice that there are no defects in the disclaimer language. The truth is that the software industry has been getting away with the delivery of unreliable software for years, and customers have been conditioned to meekly accept it "as the way things are."

In the post–year 2000 world, corporate and government executives will hopefully put an end to the practice of expending corporate and taxpayer resources on the endless task of making unreliable vendor software and systems work. Technology staffs are so accepting of this condition that it would never occur to them to even complain. But scarce corporate and government resources should not be spent on debugging programs for the software vendor, and resources should not be spending an inordinate amount of time on the care and feeding of the computer because of defects that have been passed along in the vendor's rush to get marketshare.

Executives must begin to demand performance warranties and obtain test certifications from independent third parties. They must not accept contractual language that perpetuates the unaccountability of software vendors.

After the Y2K experience, sincere and honest attention will be given to software quality because customers will have become more discerning and will be selecting providers based on their reputation for quality products and work. Contract arrangements will begin to get tougher and warranties will begin to evolve that reflect the "duty" of the IT expert to the nonexpert customer. During litigation, consequential damages will begin to be considered to a much greater degree than in pre–year 2000 days. See Appendix D.

But this movement to greater accountability for IT vendors and for other companies that supply products and services that are IT-intensive will be a two-edged sword. For example, there will be greater obligations placed on the buyer when custom software systems are to be constructed.

Essentially, buyers will be required to do a better job defining their needs. Buyers of IT products and services must clearly understand the business process improvements they wish to achieve and state such improvements in measurable terms that can form the basis of realistic specifications and contracts. Plan now for reputable IT companies to be more demanding in terms of reaching agreement as to definitions of exactly what is to be delivered. More rigor will be expected of the customer before contracts are finalized. A reputable IT company will require this increased rigor from the customer because IT risks must now be shared and they will not accept such risks alone. As the likelihood of litigation increases, look for IT companies to be more demanding as well.

OUTSOURCING: PANACEA OR POTENTIAL THREAT?

One of the questionable practices of the pre–year 2000 period, supported by compelling expectations, is the long-term wisdom of excessive outsourcing or contracting out of IT support functions. Contracting out has become the implementation strategy for downsizing initiatives and as such has added a new dimension to the threatened loss of corporate memory. Depending on which IT functions are to be contracted out, the threat may be slight or potentially catastrophic. Early candidates for contracting out centered on the repetitive and monitoring types of IT activities, such as data entry and mainframe computer operations. More recently, outsourcing agreements have included system administration and maintenance functions where vendor certification of operating personnel have provided the improved levels of proficiency needed for increasingly complex environments.

The latest IT contracting strategy is to outsource the entire information processing activity or major elements of it to the extent that dependence on contractors can become near total and very dangerous.

This latest phenomenon needs to be examined from a perspective greater than the economic arguments set forth to justify downsizing. Executives must evaluate such proposals with a keen sense of risk to the total business.

There are a great number of considerations inherent to an outsourcing evaluation and some that recap the tests of feasibility. In fact, with a comprehensive feasibility study, the proposals should include a contracting or outsourcing option for obtaining the proposed solution or service. In the feasibility study, outsourcing can first be considered during the operational examination.

But tests of feasibility, by themselves, do not always provide the scope of analysis needed to adequately address the special issues associated with outsourcing. For instance, operational feasibility does not account for the legalities and politics of outsourcing and other forms of contracting out. In recent years the prevailing climate both in business and government has been specialization and the just-in-time acquisition of resources to support the business process. Specialization means that a business or government agency decides to concentrate on performing its "core" function while acquiring IT support services and products as needed from the marketplace. For many, this means contracting out a majority of the activities that create the IT business processing environment and supporting administrative functions. This frees up, so the argument goes, the business principals to pursue their core, revenue-generating activity, be it product, service, or consultation.

The question of premier importance is what constitutes the core functions of the business and how dependent is the core on the IT activities being considered for outsourcing. For example, many local governments plan to outsource their data center, network management, applications development, and help desk services. To determine an acceptable level of contractor dependency, the core government functions must be categorized as to citizen-related criticality, and then a public service judgment needs to be made as to whether contractors can be counted on to be as responsive to public needs as would a civil service workforce. This is not an easy judgment to make politically because it questions the trend toward privatization, which has very powerful promoters. But all things being equal, the real question comes down to whether IT outsourcing contracts can be written that will provide the flexibility and responsiveness we expect of our civil servants. Or does the state of IT contracting lend itself to the demands of a situation where elected officials need to have direct control over employees, not just a contractor's project manager working within the confines of a contract that is generally written to protect the interests of the contractor.

The same question must be asked of corporate plans to outsource IT activities. If the contracted IT support function is mission-critical to the core revenue-generating business, can the company rest easy knowing that the primary recourse for obtaining the accurate and timely completion of critical IT tasks is through enforcement of a contract? Given the current state of IT warranties and contracting, this issue is of critical importance.

To examine whether IT outsourcing is appropriate in a given situation, a number of questions need to be asked.

• Can the IT activity being considered for outsourcing be defined to a degree of precision that allows measurement of the work to be contracted?

• Can these activities be controlled adequately by existing corporate technical managers, or does contract performance fall mainly to a contracting official?

• Can IT tasks that extend into the future be delineated, or are there a great many *to be determined (TBD)* actions?

• If "information" products constitute the revenue-generating core of the business, who controls that information and makes all decisions related to its generation, processing, protection, use, and final disposition?

• Is the organization structured to permit managing information as a corporate resource? Do data and information policy standards exist? Do quality standards exist, and are they measurable? Can these standards be contractually required of the outsource company, and can they be subject to audit?

• Does executive management appreciate the need for sufficient funding to require a contractor to take necessary quality assurance (QA), contingent staffing, and maintenance task-related actions to ensure proper QA, backup, and redundancy of critical processes supporting mission-critical systems, data, and information?

• Can meaningful penalties for nonperformance be levied under the contract, or are the penalties allowed merely token? Remember, the company is dealing with mission-critical support for core revenue-generating business applications. The potential for lost revenues and the potential for liability damage to business partners must be carefully considered.

• Are all business principals comfortable with the degree of corporate dependency posed by outsourcing these functions?

The critical problem faced by many organizations seeking to outsource their IT functions and activities is that they do not have the necessary policies and metrics in place or the necessary understanding of the degree of detailed specification language it takes to keep the outsource contractor responsive to the core business.

Before outsourcing, many of the details were in the heads of employees who understood the core business and its unique demands and characteristics. These employees were perhaps present when the system was built or were at least answerable to the same corporate leadership. With outsourcing, all these relationships and system nuances must be reduced to the language of contracts. It is significant to note that contract negotiations become very complicated as businesses struggle with how to structure and manage their outsourcing deals. Outsourcing merely because the task has become a headache for the company only results in a bigger headache once contract officials and lawyers have to become involved. If the task was a headache for a company, it may well prove to be a major problem for the outsource contractor as well. The reasons IT was difficult for an organization to cope with do not disappear because an outsourcer is now tasked to do the same work under a contract arrangement.

Another, and even worse, reason to outsource is the claim that the existing internal IT support group does not know what needs to be done or how to do it. An organization must at least know, perhaps by way of independent consultation, what IT functions need to be performed and have a working knowledge of how to accomplish those functions. Without such knowledge, the outsourcer will indeed have total control over the contracted activity and eventually over the company.

SHORT-TERM ECONOMICS VS. SUSTAINABLE SYSTEMS

As discussed previously, an economic cost/benefit or ROI analysis should be conducted only after technical feasibility and operational feasibility have been evaluated carefully. The reason for this is essentially the need to go overboard to determine all the cost consequences of a course of IT action. For years system planners, seeking to formulate an understanding of the consequences of a technology path, have had to overcome the *tyranny of the hardware cost curve.* All too often, the exponential decline in the cost of computer hardware has been the primary driving force behind many system decisions. This cost-curve reduction, variously expressed as cost per unit of memory, cost per unit of data transferred, or cost per executed instruction, while duly impressive, gives a very one-sided and incomplete picture of the total cost of system ownership. The cost of ownership is a comprehensive and much more accurate measure of what an IT initiative will cost over the life of the system. Therefore, it provides insight into the long-term expenses associated not only with purchasing or building a system but with sustaining it as well.

If the short-term economics of a bargain-basement systems project is gaining momentum, then special efforts must be taken to identify all associated system sustainability costs accurately. A partial list was provided in Exhibit 2.1, and each of these categories can be broken down further for greater detail. These costs will give a better understanding of sustaining costs, but even these do not address the hidden costs of doing business in today's technology environment.

Before closing out the Y2K cleanup and moving on to the technologies of the next decade, be alert to the following hidden costs of doing the business of IT. Each cost is real and must somehow be factored into overall system sustainability calculations.

• The ever-increasing cost of making complex heterogenous IT environments work together. The promise of user-friendly, better, and faster are products of marketing departments. Reality is a different matter. When e-mail attachments are difficult to master, when PCs and networks still are unreliable and crash several times a week, the cost of doing the business of IT can be substantial. Again, the need for the gathering of metrics data becomes clear. As long as even the simplest measures of uptime, time to repair, mean time between failure, and others are not known, hidden costs will remain hidden and the true cost of ownership will never be calculable.

• The indifference of many IT service providers, software vendors, and on-line service companies to providing responsive after-sale support, even when paid for, leads to a loss of employee productivity within a company. A vast number of IT provider companies view support as an add-on service and seem to understand nothing of customer relations. To add insult to injury, the failure of software vendors to deliver quality and warrantable products has even been turned into an additional revenue stream as customers are given (900) numbers to call for information on how to make the software function. This inattention to usable customer documentation is supported by the fact that all major software user instructions are confusing enough to have spawned an entire publishing industry of "how-to" and "for Dummies" training manuals. Vendors do not spend enough effort communicating how to productively use the software or system just built or purchased for employees to be successful. To guarantee organizational success, these initial and continuing hidden training expenses must be recognized and factored in as a cost of doing the business of IT.

• Breakdowns in IT systems and support services directly impact the bottom line of the business. The more the business depends on IT, the more consequential any breakdown will be and the more the hidden costs of doing the business of IT will accumulate. Collecting data concerning breakdowns and related revenue losses will, in the future, give support to those who argue for system processing protections, redundancies, and appropriate backup and continency planning. As web-based technologies put more businesses on-line, it will be important to have access to such metrics for use when selecting Internet providers or any other IT outsource contractor.

• Forced upgrades enrich vendors and cost a company dearly. Software vendors, PC makers, telecos, Internet service providers, electronic commerce providers, and their investors are all in search of the pot of gold at the end of the rainbow. Revenues must be generated continually at a faster and faster pace. Since *brute* processing capacities and speeds keep improving at ever-decreasing costs, the stage is set to create new software applications to use the increased capacity. New applications and their demands soon accumulate and require yet greater processing capacities and speeds. This interdependent cycle between these two elements of the IT industry conspire effectively to force a business into what is marketed as an upgrade-or-lose-competitive-advantage situation. Many IT-intensive organizations increasingly recognize that software vendors really run their company. Whenever revenues need to increase at the vendor software company, they plan new products and announce a new release. These come at regular intervals of 18 months to two years, but may or may not affect using a company that frequently. But within every three to four years the vendor will announce that systems being used to run a business will no longer be supported and an IT organization is encouraged to upgrade to the most recent appropriate release. This begins a series of expensive hardware, software, integration, and migration projects that may or may not add any appreciable value to the way a company does business or to the bottom line.

Forced upgrades would not be so bad if a business had to deal with only the visible costs, but hidden costs result every time upgrades are announced.

JUST-IN-TIME DESIGNS: WEAKEST LINK THREAT TO BUSINESS VIABILITY?

To a great extent, the prosperity of the late 1990s can be attributed directly to the successful use of computers to reduce operating inventories and the traditional expense associated with warehousing. The design of just-in-time manufacturing and distribution systems would not be possible without the close integration of many different IT systems up and down a supply chain. The essence of a just-in-time application is the rapid and accurate exchange of order entry data, inventory status data, manufacturing data, raw materials and parts data, and shipping status data among multiple corporations held together by a common desire to succeed in business and reduce costs. The nature of a just-in-time system is one of mutual dependency and is only as strong as the "weakest" link in the chain of systems. Great efficiencies have been realized through just-in-time architectures, and they will continue to be central to the business model of the future. There are, however, many risks inherent in such designs, and care must be taken to identify vulnerabilities that could incapacitate a link so that actions can be taken to mitigate such threats.

Just-in-time business arrangements must be supported by carefully designed automated systems that span across many different organizations. This is a task far too important to leave to the various corporate IT departments. Just-in-time designs invoke a multitude of organizational interactions each time the system is activated. Each corporate link in the chain has a responsibility to all other links according to predefined contractual obligations. It is imperative that these obligations be spelled out in business– and technical service–level agreements incorporated into those contractual arrangements. Service-level agreements are negotiated definitions, with metrics for measurement, that spell out the exact required technical interactions that must occur for a just-in-time business transaction to be considered successful. To a great extent, a just-in-time business design requires a multiorganizational feasibility study accomplished jointly. The essential actions leading to just-in-time service level agreements should include:

• The establishment of an intercompany business process review executive committee to ensure the mutual benefit of each partner to the supply chain and to establish the business process service–level agreements that are to be reflected in contracts between companies.

• The establishment of technical support review committees that report to the business process review executive committee to ensure that the hardware, software, and communications infrastructure to support the business service–level agreement are designed properly and are sufficient to the task.

• A joint design of the business process to be executed among the individual supply chain partners. This should include agreement and standardization of data element representations to be exchanged and clear definitions of what each element of data means across the supply chain.

• Timing of transactions from initiation to final product delivery need to be stated clearly and concisely and subjected to a feasibility review and security assessment.

• Problem scenarios need to be developed and problem resolution procedures established that are periodically exercised. Scenarios should include potential disruptions to the just-in-time process flow that provide guidance to business continuity planning efforts.

• Since supply chain disruptions can virtually destroy a just-in-time manufacturing and/or distribution business and result in substantial revenue loss, a business interruption and security risk analysis (i.e., cost vs. loss study) should be conducted to justify any necessary extra expenses needed to build a supply chain system with quick recovery characteristics.

Such actions, in the post–year 2000 environment, will require the direct involvement of the most senior executives. These are issues and questions of corporate survivability that can no longer be delegated without frequent, active, and documented executive review. The Y2K experience and its aftermath means that stockholders, employees, and the board will expect this level of executive involvement.

HAVING A QUALITY ASSURANCE STAFF IS NOT ENOUGH

The assumption that it is enough to have a quality assurance staff with its associated expectation of quality systems and software, serves to illustrate an underlying reality about IT brought to awareness by the recent Y2K experience. At a knowledge level, the IT industry knows how to build systems that satisfy all of the characteristics normally thought of as belonging to quality software or systems. Even though the Y2K data problem originated from an early design efficiency decision (i.e., saving two digits of storage every time a date was entered by recording only the last two digits), the industry never was especially challenged by the technical measures required to fix it. And the industry, in the abstract, would have been able to do a better job of engineering the fix if work had been started earlier and if QA techniques had been employed during system remediation. In fact, it can be argued that fully implemented QA programs would have prevented the perpetuation of two-digit coding in the first place through the exercise of inspection and reviews.

The reality is that while the IT industry knows how to build quality systems, circumstances have conspired, in most organizations, against that happening.

The introductory paragraphs of Appendix D list the terms most often used to define quality of software and systems. These "quality attributes" can be thought of as "adjectives" that modify the software or systems "noun." Quality attributes specify measurable characteristics that a finished software or a system must possess in order to meet the business requirements they are designed to support. Without quality attributes that are accurately specified, software and system developers do not know the tolerances within which the final product must operate. Once defined, quality attributes guide the design and development effort and become the foundation for testing.

Using the example of Y2K, the software requirement *calculate date,* needed to be modified by a quality attribute requirement for accuracy that specified "into, through, and beyond" the century turnover, further qualified by the modifier "accurately accounting for leap years." Without this particular quality attribute being defined for date calculations, programmers unintentionally were allowed to overlook the century date problem for years. Without this specification for what constituted accurate date processing, there was no date focus during testing, and so the problem remained undiscovered except for those few who were somehow enlightened to the issue.

Most QA staffs, and the organizational programs with which they are associated, are of two kinds. They are either advisory in nature and consultive in the scope of their involvement with actual software or systems projects or they perform a quality control function near the end of a development effort where they conduct tests on nearly finished products. Neither role is what quality assurance is about, and neither provides executives with the reassurances that quality is being built into software or system. Quality assurance focuses on the processes used during software and systems development and incorporates quality-promoting techniques throughout those processes.

Consultive and advisory QA efforts are helpful as far as they go, but they cannot truly affect the final outcome of a development unless someone is actually responsible to deliver a quality product. And since responsibility needs to be accompanied by the necessary and equal authority to make decisions and allocate resources, the task of ensuring quality necessarily resides with the line manager whose business process will be supported by the software or system. Only in this way can the necessary decisions be made that will prevent the circumvention of QA techniques that has occurred so often when IT alone was viewed as responsible but given insufficient authority to build quality into business support systems. In practice, this means that QA must be considered an integral element of the development process with activities occurring at all phases of the development process. (See Appendix B for a discussion on the integration of QA into a generic systems development process [SDP] model.)

From an executive perspective, management for QA effectiveness comes down to the proper identification and monitoring of certain key metrics. The foremost of these metrics deals with the cost of quality. Similar to the cost of quality used in manufacturing, or with another product that is process dependent, the cost of quality for software and systems is related directly to when in the development process an error or requirements

Exhibit 3.1   Relative Cost to Fix an Error or Omission

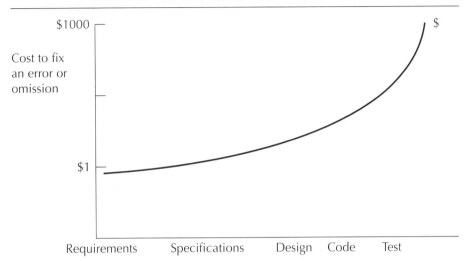

omission is detected. The cost to correct an error or add a requirement is low in the early stages of development but grows exponentially as the project progresses. The relative cost to fix an error or correct a requirements omission at each phase of software development is shown in Exhibit 3.1.

This curve can be viewed as a cost of quality progression because the final product will be thought of as being a quality product, but at what cost? The earlier in the development process an error or omission can be detected, the less it will cost to correct—thus ensuring that quality is attained. The later in the development process an error or omission is detected, the more it will cost to correct—thus ensuring that quality is attained. Both situations illustrate the cost of producing a quality product.

The first analysis of this reality resulted from the seminal work of Barry Boehm in 1976. Dr. Vern Crandell collected the data in Exhibit 3.2 between 1982 and 1985. They reinforced the earlier findings of Boehm. The guidelines portrayed the cost of finding errors at various points in the software development life cycle.

Exhibit 3.3 portrays the range of potential dollar amounts experienced by multiple companies.

To be sure, these dollar amounts are not the only costs associated with the cost of attaining quality, but they serve to indicate problems in the management of software and systems development. They adversely affect the

Exhibit 3.2   Cost of Finding Errors at Various Points in the Software Development Life Cycle

Company	Specif. design	Programming	Testing	Install. & Maint.
IBM/Raleigh	$10	$100	$1,000	$25,000
IBM/Rochester				$8000 ($10,000)
Large LA firm		$900	$19,000	$19,000
Hewlett-Packard	1 unit	10 units	100 units	
IBM/Santa Teresa	1 unit	27 units	64 units	127 units

Source: Adapted from Vern Crandall, Ph.D., private consultant to Sun Microsystems. *The Cost of Effectiveness of Software Testing Making a Case to Management* (Mountain View, Calif.: Sun Microsystems, Inc., 1992), 45.

bottom line. These amounts point to deficiencies in the procedures and processes being used to develop and field software and systems and function as a barometer of the effectiveness and efficiency of those development efforts.

These amounts, however, are only the tip of the iceberg. They reflect only the cost to finally achieve some degree of software or systems quality from an IT perspective. They do not begin to account for the costs borne by the business user or customer in trying to work with and work around systems whose defects are not discovered until after deployment to the workplace. They do not account for revenues that are lost while the system is unavailable for use. They do not account for the lost productivity of employees during the average 7 to 10 percent local area network downtime experienced daily by the average business. These unrecognized effects are especially acute where systems are integral to just-in-time business applications. With many businesses, the quality of their goods and services are linked directly to the quality of the automated information and the trust that can be placed in the integrity of the support systems.

A lack of quality information and a loss of trust in the integrity of underlying business processes can contribute to deficient enterprise decisions, poor-quality work products, and poor customer service.

For example, at the direct customer contact level, an inaccurate address for a package delivery service company, resulting in late delivery, contributes to a poor image for the company and, if service was guaranteed, the potential for legal action. At the middle management level, inaccurate

Exhibit 3.3   Guidelines for the Cost of Fixing Errors Across the Software Development Life Cycle

	Specif. Design	Programming	Testing	Install. & Maint.
Guidelines	$10–$100	$100–$300	$500–$1500	$10,000–millions

Source: Adapted from Vern Crandall, Ph.D., private consultant to Sun Microsystems. *The Cost of Effectiveness of Software Testing Making a Case to Management* (Mountain View, Calif.: Sun Microsystems, Inc., 1992), 46.

or incomplete information about required staffing skills may lead to poor recruitments that ultimately threaten a project's timely completion. Again, the company's reputation suffers. Finally, at the executive planning level, poor data collection and analysis, due to defective software, concerning a new technology and the stability of potential suppliers result in late implementation of a new product or service. The corporation loses a hoped-for competitive advantage and wastes limited resources. None of the dollar amounts in Exhibits 3.2 and 3.3 reflect such losses, yet in the world of quality management all such costs are accounted for and calculated into an overall cost of quality profile.

Those exhibits also illustrate the fate that overtakes software and system developments that have not embraced and implemented full quality assurance programs. Sooner or later such development efforts are overwhelmed by an avalanche of errors. Exhibit 3.4 depicts the cumulative effect of not having sufficient quality assurance in place and enforced to detect problems throughout each phase of the development. The quality assurance techniques of independent validation, verification, and test provide a check that the processes used in systems construction are meeting requirements using best practice design and programming techniques. Independent validation, verification, and testing ensure that other quality improvement techniques, such as walkthroughs, code inspections, and documentation reviews, are being performed and that testing of code at the module, subsystem, and systems level is being conducted.

Quality assurance initiatives, properly staffed and empowered with authority as well as responsibility, can provide great improvements in the quality management of IT projects. Once the metrics of quality (i.e., numbers of errors, omissions, and defect resolution statistics) are established and kept for a reasonable period of time, management will be able to iden-

Exhibit 3.4   Avalanche of Errors

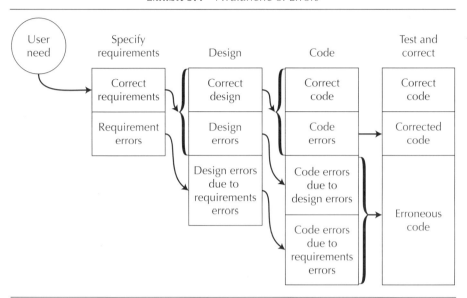

tify development process problem areas and take corrective action. In this way, long-term improvements can be made to the business of IT and executives will begin to see the sort of measurement data long available from other aspects of the business.

THE QUALITY ETHIC OF IT AND BUSINESS IMPACT

Many of those recovering from the consequences of the Y2K data problem are angry not so much because of the glitch itself but because of the way they feel they were treated by the IT industry as a whole. And the anger is not directed solely at their Y2K experience but at the sum of their IT experiences over the years. As a growth industry, surrounded by mystery, pumped up by endless hype, where fortunes have been easily made and where metrics do not exist or cannot provide sufficient intelligence with which to establish control, IT has evolved a take-it-or-leave-it attitude that leaves little room for the satisfied customer.

Here is how one end user summed up the systems development process: "Let me tell you what I've come to expect from systems development projects: They take twice as long as promised, cost twice as much as anticipated, and produce half the functionality they were designed for in the first place."*

Many in IT probably would say that this end user had a reasonably good experience. And as Exhibit 1.2 indicated, users generally are dissatisfied and oftentimes are greatly inconvenienced by the introduction of technology into their workplace. They are dissatisfied because the technology system often does not substantially assist in improving the efficiency or the effectiveness of their job performance and seldom lives up to what was promised. They are inconvenienced because all too often users must devise workarounds to keep the business functioning despite the technical system.

The litany of publicized system failures is well documented. Then came the Y2K problem and the IT industry's response to it. We must differentiate at this point between IT product suppliers (i.e., hardware, software, package software vendors, etc.) and IT integrators, or support service contractors, who attempted to pull all the vendor-compliant, ready, and compliant-capable products together so businesses could continue to function. Integrators, support service contractors, and a firm's own IT employees often accomplished wonders, given the poor record of some IT suppliers to get their products Y2K compliant. It is no wonder that many corporations suffered at the hands of IT product suppliers. With an industry that regularly passes "buggy" codes off onto customers, looks to customers to become the end product testers, and then forces customers to purchase upgraded software containing fixes to bugs found by customers, why should the Y2K bug have been handled any differently?

A more serious question for corporate executives to ponder is to what degree this IT quality ethic has adversely affected the way their company does business. In what ways have the poor quality of software from IT suppliers compromised a company's commitment to customer satisfaction and quality service? How often must a company, its employees, and its customers bear the consequence of software and system failures? How much of the IT support staff's time is spent recovering from and working around defects that should have been discovered by the developer during testing and before the product was released for sale? Remember that Exhibits 3.1,

*Daniel Borgen and Michael Silverman, "Manager's Journal," *ComputerWorld* (Feb. 19, 1991): 45.

3.2, and 3.3 reflect only the costs that are experienced by the software or system developer to correct a problem after its discovery. One can only speculate on the dollar losses experienced by thousands of businesses that encounter the same software failures and must wait for the developer to create a solution and release a software fix. Data of this type gathered by Paul Straussman, independent consultant and former Assistant Secretary of Defense, indicates productivity losses due to bad software to be many millions of dollars annually. But no one knows for sure.

What recourse do businesses have to counter this state of affairs?

EXERCISE THE CUSTOMER SATISFACTION PARADIGM: DEMAND QUALITY

Quality management advocates often use the customer satisfaction paradigm as the driving force behind the adoption of quality assurance and continuous improvement initiatives. In practice, this means that businesses have tended to concentrate on pleasing their customers upon whom they depend for sales and revenue. As may be suspected, this approach presupposes an element of control over the products and services to be delivered that may not exist when, in fact, those products and services are heavily dependent on external IT suppliers and vendors. Poor-quality IT software and systems, upon which many businesses rely, make it unduly difficult to keep corporate commitments to customer satisfaction. A familiar example of this would be the blame that airlines endure when air traffic control systems experience problems and slowdowns are activated. The solution to this problem is to start exercising corporate muscle and options as a customer. Today's corporation may seem to be at the mercy of IT product and service providers, but this can change. The way to begin is to systematically manage internal IT departments and IT suppliers the way any other business relationship would be managed.

First, stop accepting the "best-effort" mentality and excuses of IT and begin to gather metrics that can be used in monitoring project status, process improvements, and negotiating service-level agreements and contracts.

Second, require accountability from IT staff and suppliers for their estimates and promises. Be sure to recognize that current IT staff and suppliers did not set all the fires they are now forced to fight; but do begin requiring accountability, as soon as possible, through the use of metrics and adherence to a system development process on all new projects.

Third, make executive displeasure known to IT suppliers directly. With a few notable exceptions, IT product and service suppliers are living close to the financial edge. They need the firm's business and will do almost anything to accommodate demands for quality software and systems. In fact, a firm may be doing the executive management of the software or services company a favor. By taking a strong position and being a demanding customer, the company may be providing the necessary ammunition to the non-IT directors of the technology company to take pro-quality measures that have long been stymied by their technology managers. Or if non-IT directors are the source of the problem, the stance may convince them to better balance the promises of their marketing and sales force against the time and effort spent on quality assurance and test activities.

Many software development companies have what may be a self-defeating attitude regarding quality versus their perception of the importance of time to market. It has long been an argument, against comprehensive testing, that a competitor will get to market first if too much time is spent on quality assurance and testing. This thinking can be altered only by customers who are willing to reward the conscientious software developer with their business and stop being the unwilling tester and guinea pig for developers who cut corners on quality during product development.

Fourth, demand that lawyers negotiate better terms than those presented by the software and service supplier. Require milestones and intermediate work deliverables for all custom software and system efforts. Demand that the developer follow an industry-recognized system development process that is heavily influenced by quality assurance activities. And until packaged software contractual and warranty terms become more reasonable, refuse to buy the first release of any new software unless it is for laboratory or test experimentation. Let others push the envelope and risk the disruptions caused by putting new software into operation before it is ready.

Finally, give quality a chance and reward those employees and those suppliers who strive, in action as well as words, for customer satisfaction.

REVENGE OF THE NERDS: OR THINK BEFORE SPEAKING

Having just been wheeled into the operating room for emergency open-heart surgery, the patient looks up at the attending cardiac physician and, before being put under, mutters, "I hope you quacks don't take too long and, by the way, I don't want to spend too much," or words to that effect. Not too smart, you say, to ridicule people who have your life in their hands. And yet, how does our culture, and yes, even business executives often refer to computer people? Do terms "nerd," "geek," "dweeb," and "propeller-head" come to mind? How are computer people depicted in the movies and in popular fiction? Does the overweight antisocial programmer of *Jurassic Park* come to view, or is it the shy high school student who saves the world in *War Games?* While the sophisticated computer criminal, à la Robert Redford in *Sneakers,* who stumbles upon a dastardly government plot and saves the republic is the very rare exception, generally computer people are presented as reclusive, out of the mainstream, highly intelligent, unattractive, immature, and more than a little weird. What are we to make of this portrayal of people on which so much depends? How can we deride computer people while we turn our business, government, and society over to them? The only other profession that enjoys such negative attention are the lawyers of jokes; but even lawyers are sometimes portrayed as heroes. Certainly, they are not ridiculed by us when we get into a legal scrap and need their assistance. They are suddenly our friends.

Computer people are not generally portrayed as anything we would want our daughters to marry—unless, of course, they manage to become a second Bill Gates. Computer people are more often closely associated with the Three Stooges or the absentminded professor; and yet we are all becoming, to some extent, computer people. What to make of this phenomenon? What impact do these prevailing images have on managerial and executive relations with computer people? The author vividly remembers the computer people in his information services division referred to as "crybaby technicians" by an executive vice president at a senior staff meeting. This was his perception of the people who managed and controlled his computers, his software systems, his ability to communicate to his nationwide empire, and his very sensitive and proprietary databases. A statement such as this may not be as openly expressed in many organizations, but this view is not atypical behind closed doors. Executives need to be sensitive to what they say and be concerned about the impact of such comments on their computer and other technical employees. Interestingly, the senior executive just quoted had, in his earlier days, been a computer technician but had decided to move on to a financial career. What can be the fallout from such perceptions, and why does it matter?

No one enjoys second-class citizen status, and we all like to be appreciated. People in the computer industry are no different. Even though executive management may not acknowledge the critical nature of their contribution, computer people know what it is and understand the power they wield. One disgruntled IT employee can cause great damage; a united disgruntled team can destroy a company. And interestingly, such harm does not necessarily require overt action. Very often it can be accomplished through conscious inaction, for example, the failure to share vital information concerning a project, a developing problem, or a troubled customer. Unhappy IT employees can wreak havoc in many ways. Since so much they do is unknown, management contemplating such things can experience sleepless nights.

Many in the IT community will laugh off the disparaging comment or stereotype classification of "nerd." Some actually take pride in such designations and enjoy that status, especially at high school reunion time when it seems that they are doing quite well while the football hero is found to be driving a truck. But to others, such disparaging comments and stereotypical portrayal serve as a "red flag" and prompts them to establish their superiority through unacceptable and illegal avenues of expression.

During the summer of 1999 there were an unprecedented number of "hacker" attacks against critical government systems such as the White House Internet site and the FBI's site. And earlier in 1999 it was acknowledged that there had been thousands of attempted penetrations against Department of Defense computers. In the private sector, industry associations also acknowledged sabotage against corporate IT capabilities to be on the rise. And contrary to popular belief, not all of these attacks are coming from adventuresome teenagers. At least some percent seem to be organized attempts to discover weaknesses in the target organization's computing environment for future exploitation. It is likely that government and corporate insiders are being actively recruited for espionage purposes. This was evidenced by the 1999 revelations alleging the loss of weapons and defense secrets to the Chinese from the Oak Ridge and Sandia National Laboratories. Computer people have been the targets of recruitment attempts aimed at gaining internal sensitive information from their current employers.

In these instances, a key element of an effective security program, especially in the case of sabotage, is the goodwill and alertness of the rest of the IT workforce. Additionally, commonsense management practice would indicate the need to "double-team" employees working in especially sensitive or potentially harmful positions.

Often, computer people believe that they are expendable and are merely commodities to be used up by the executive suite. These feelings are usually reinforced when they are repeatedly expected to commit to what software expert and author of over 20 IT books Ed Yourdon refers to as death-march projects. Death-march projects, with their ridiculous expectations and insane time frames, are dictated by executives who exhibit a "burn 'em up and throw 'em away" attitude. Eventually, this will drive employees away from the corporation. Usually, the best people leave first— they know insanity when they see it—and they then recruit the rest of the staff to get bonus money from their new employer.

As ill-advised as these human resources practices appear, they are downright suicidal given the fact that corporation and government agencies do not enforce the documentation requirements of their systems development methodologies and often do not plan for task continuity in the event an employee leaves.

There seems to be a serious disconnect in the minds of executives and middle-level management between their near-total dependence on computer people and any rational strategy for managing the risks posed by that dependence. And yet, the disparaging language and jokes continue.

RESPONSIBILITY/AUTHORITY AND THE SUCCESS OF IT

The failure to align responsibility with concomitant authority is a reality of organizational life that adversely affected the successful resolution of the recent Y2K problem. This problem also has significant implications for the post–year 2000 uses of IT. It is not uniquely related to IT but certainly will adversely affect the future success of information technology uses within contemporary organizations if not addressed.

This reality recognizes the dichotomy between constructing systems of increasingly greater complexity that require great integration across organizational lines and the limited accountability effectiveness of most organizational structures. Even project management structures have minimal effectiveness in such cases because line management will outlive the influence of the project manager. Integral to this reality are the questions of centralization versus decentralization. Put simply, who is accountable for the successful use of IT to support the business, and does the organizational structure and system of rewards and consequences support that assignment of accountability? Actually, except at the worker level, is there an effective system of rewards and consequences, or have "golden parachutes" essentially done away with the concept of consequences and therefore with effective accountability?

Single-point accountability must be fixed especially if the system crosses organizational lines and extends to business partners and suppliers.

Often, one of the first mistakes that is made is to assign responsibility for an IT project to a committee of representatives from the impacted areas. Committees are fine for gathering requirements, studying proposals, and preparing their respective organizations for implementation. Committees, however, cannot be substituted for having overall project responsibility reside in one directed line manager.

The second mistake is to place responsibility with a staff or special projects officer, usually chosen because of executive affiliations and loyalties; or with an executive staff officer, not of the line, such as the chief information officer (CIO). Executive staff officers such as CIOs, audit groups, comptrollers, and general counsel can provide guidance, perform studies, provide justifications, conduct audits, and the like, but they do not have authority to change work priorities and allocate resources between competing production demands. They do not manage the factors of production and are not responsible for revenues. Only line or business unit managers have such authority, for this reason, responsibility for "making it happen" must rest with them.

In a past life, the author was recruited by a very large and well-known government agency to develop and implement a nationwide program. The program, systems security, dealt with all automated as well as manual processing systems executed by over 80,000 employees. The agency had been recently criticized by oversight committees and auditors for the lack of a coherent policy and strategic plan for implementing security controls across the organization. The agency was organized into a very large headquarters operation with over a dozen associate commissioners, each reporting to the commissioner. Field operations were organized into another dozen regional headquarters each with a regional commissioner and several large geographic service centers each headed by a senior director. The author, from a headquarters staff position, many layers removed from the commissioner, was given responsibility for agencywide systems security. Creation of this position and especially the recruitment from outside quieted the auditors so criticism abated for a while. With a staff of 10 and with no authority over the field or the computer systems that needed securing, we did all that could be done from a powerless staff position—we educated, held conferences, "floated" policies that went nowhere, and generally made pests of ourselves.

Then, 18 months after creation of the systems security staff, a series of major embarrassments arose stemming from employees' accessing, for amusement purposes, the files of prominent individuals in payment status. The oversight groups and the auditors rejuvenated themselves and wondered why the system security program had not prevented such a thing. At that time, the commissioner became aware that much he had been hearing, from his associate and regional commissioners, was just rhetoric; they had not taken many of the security measures they had talked about. The commissioner, a political appointee, learned that trying to get some things done on the basis of collegiality is just not sufficient. Stronger measures are required. When asked, I recommended that he place the responsibility for systems security into the annual merit pay contracts of appropriate senior executives and use it as one of their performance review items. In this way, responsibility for secured agency systems was assigned to the only people who could "make it happen," and the commissioner made it clear where his priorities were. Much to my surprise, the commissioner took my advice. I had essentially talked myself out of a job, but it was the only way that a cross-cutting organizational issue such as security was going to get implemented.

The same approach needs to be taken now to begin to get accountability into the corporate use of IT. Unless line and business unit managers are held directly accountable for the successful implementation of the next IT initiative, they will continue to do that for which they are being rewarded— and that probably is not something that is considered to be an IT function.

Other examples of the importance of aligning responsibility and authority can be found with the recent Y2K experience. Again, the author can relate personal experience functioning as a consultant to a CIO given responsibility for the Y2K project. As is typical, the CIO had no line authority and a small staff to carry out all the other duties of a chief information officer. The chief executive officer (CEO), the board of directors, the shareholders, auditors, and assistants all expected the CIO to fulfill her responsibility to save the organization from the bug. Except for the mainframe folks, no one else really understood the far-reaching business implications of the bug and the adverse impacts it could have on the organization as a whole and on those clients receiving monthly payments. The only organizational vehicle that existed to accomplish the required work was a steering committee made up of volunteers who, more or less, had expressed an interest and possible concern about the topic. Two natural leaders emerged from the committee, but neither could speak for, nor commit, their bosses. This is the perfect bureaucratic response to a problem no one ever really wishes to address, much less solve. But Y2K was different; it had a deadline—it could not be delayed. With less than two years remaining, the challenge for the CIO was to "get everyone onto the Y2K hook."

The solution was to identify the major compliance actions that needed to take place and then convince the CEO to formally place the responsibility with those executives possessing the direct authority to "make it happen." For example, many operations depended on IT software and hardware vendors and third-party contractors, such as insurance carriers and contract physicians. All of these business partners and suppliers needed to be contacted to determine their level of compliance. Rather than expect each element of the organization to contact their business partners and suppliers, it was noted that each relationship was legally established in a license or a contract. Therefore, it was decided that all business partner and supplier contracts would be the responsibility of the contracts official.

In all, 15 individual Y2K master program elements were identified, and the CEO named 7 executive offices to be responsible for the implementation of those programs assigned to them. These assignments were to *offices,* not to individuals. This kept all actions within a legal framework necessary to show due diligence. Each office was then required to report monthly to the CEO on progress against the plan.

Both of these examples accomplished one other important thing. By aligning authority with responsibility and by having these actions directed by the commissioner and the CEO, a mantle of protection was placed over my boss in the first case and over my client in the Y2K example. These actions denied both the commissioner and the CEO the comfort of plausible deniability, although in both instances that was probably not possible because of the highly visible nature of the underlying problem to be solved.

The successful use of IT in a post–year 2000 world is going to demand that executives take control of the playing field and dictate the rules of engagement. These rules are not unlike what would be expected when pursuing any other corporate undertaking. There is a discipline to managing IT, and commonsense elements of this discipline have been mentioned. In the appendixes, other essential elements of this discipline are presented to assist executives with the management of IT in the years ahead.

IT THROUGH ROSE-COLORED GLASSES

No doubt, the first description of seeing the world through rose-colored glasses was the "power of positive thinking" by Dr. Norman Vincent Peale. Over the years, many similar phrases have evolved that further the notion that with an optimistic outlook, all obstacles can be overcome and anything is possible if it is only believed in strongly enough. Most purveyors of these sentiments work in the human potential and self-actualization world and never met Mr. Murphy of "if anything can go wrong, it will" fame. They probably never talked to Mr. Speer about his first Law of Proofreading: "The visibility of an error is inversely proportional to the number of times you have looked for it."

Executives who view the world through rose-colored glasses unwittingly demonstrate to IT people, and other engineering types, that they are likely to be disciples of Mr. Weiler and his law, which states, "Nothing is impossible for the man who doesn't have to do it himself." Likewise, such executives take too little notice of Mr. Ducharme and his axiom, which states, "If you view your problem closely enough you will recognize yourself as part of the problem."

Rose-colored glasses executives or managers can be dangerous to the successful use of informational and other technologies because they project an image of being oblivious, or uncaring, to the problems and complexities facing the system's developer. They actually may know better, but projecting this image can lull people into a false sense of security (i.e., how could the executive be so confident and upbeat if there were any substantial problems?) while sending a message of "nonurgency" or "nonimportance" to the technicians who need to sense executive objectivity and realism when asked to resolve problems of competing priorities.

DEALING WITH THE REALITY OF TECHNOLOGICAL PROBLEMS

Making allowances for the necessity of public relations pronouncements to citizens and employees about how great the future is always going to be, what could account for business and government's failure to come to grips with the large number of systemic problems facing all of us—problems that run the gamut from the conditions of the nation's schools, to the crumbling of city infrastructures, to the safety of nuclear waste disposal? Are these simply more instances of rose-colored glasses management?

First Denial

Observers of humanity claim that we, as a species, demonstrate a difficult time accepting long-term responsibility for our actions and inactions. Our focus seems to be very, very short, next year at most, next season most probably. In business, reward systems are based on quarterly report profit-and-loss statements. It takes great effort to convince management of the necessity to forgo some profit today to invest resources on the longer-term issues of quality development, infrastructure maintenance, and operational stability. And yet, the more interdependent society's systems become, the more essential it will be to invest in the long-term issues of the supporting infrastructure. This is especially true when addressing problems related to IT systems. With regard to the Y2K problem, this fundamental failing has again been demonstrated for all to see.

At first most companies and governments denied that such a problem even existed, and a great deal of valuable time was lost trying to convince people there was indeed a threat. In fact, anyone open to an hour of education and discussion concerning the matter became convinced of a threat, in the abstract, but did not necessarily believe it could ever affect them or their business. Another few hours of education and discussion and another level of threat realization would be achieved. But denial, at the personal impact level, usually retarded progress toward acceptance of Y2K as a problem requiring action. After much education and many, many discussions, the threat finally may have been acknowledged, but what to do?

More time now elapsed as management and organizations became educated on how to tackle the problem and what resources would be needed. Next, plans had to be formulated and budgets developed.

Procrastination

In most of these instances, organizations were attempting to solve a time-sensitive and critical problem by using the same routine bureaucratic methods employed on all previous IT projects. Emergency budgets and acquisitions were initially discouraged, and more time elapsed as resources were gathered out of current operating budget allocations to attack the problem. Procrastination in the face of a nonnegotiable end date is hard to fathom, and yet apparently that is what occurred in many organizations as they adopted a wait-and-see attitude. Procrastination on most other IT projects, however, is simply due to the desire to not spend money. Procrastination is the other human tendency that, when coupled with denial, results in the imposition on employees of impossible workloads to be completed in dangerously short time frames, thereby risking a full spectrum of undesirable effects, from low-quality work products to mass employee defections. All this occurs because short-term reward systems do not support the long-term commitments required to build quality systems that are stable and capable of being maintained over their anticipated life.

Followed by "Not My Job"

By this time, any systems project is already behind the eight-ball. Precious time has been lost during the first two phases, and now progress has to be made and made quickly. Also, by now internal company bureaucrats have determined whether the project has any real chance of success. If no one expresses an interest in managing or mentoring the undertaking, probably it has been deemed a career buster. Experienced bureaucrats either will suggest reaching down into the organization for a project manager, or they will suggest hiring someone from outside the company. In either case, they will be able to look out for their own interests, keeping their personal risk at a minimum.

Lining Up the Scapegoat

Only when the project finally moves forward under direction of an elevated insider or an outside hire does meaningful analysis actually get accomplished. By now the project is months behind the expectations of senior executives who only remember the wishful-thinking time lines that originally were presented during the denial and procrastination phases.

It now falls to the new project manager to play one and perhaps two roles as the project progresses. The Scott Adams cartoon (Exhibit 3.5) portrays both roles and certainly proves the adage that a picture is worth a thousand words. As messenger, the project manager eventually must deliver the word that all is not well with the project, due primarily to the time that has been wasted as the organization went through the denial and procrastination phases and while people were jockeying for bureaucratic position and career advantage. If the project manager survives on the project for any length of time, and if anything goes wrong, he or she fills the role of scapegoat.

These are some of the reasons project managers, even those deemed successful by the organization, seek the sanctuary of technical, nonmanagerial work following their project experience. Knowing when to get involved with a project and when to move on is an art that is mastered over time.

Refusing to listen to the very experts who were hired is more evidence of never having left the denial phase of the problem's progression. As Scott Adams continually points out, there are plenty of reasons for managers

Exhibit 3.5

DILBERT reprinted by permission of United Feature Syndicate, Inc.

who do not want to deal with problems and never a shortage of well-meaning, but naive, targets to shoot.

CONCLUSION

It seems advisable to reflect on known difficulties if future improvements are to be made and mistakes are not to be repeated. To be sure IT is, by any standard, a young industry in the throes of very rapid change and immense innovation. But it is an industry that for the most part does not exist for itself. Storing, processing, and communicating 0s and 1s, the coded representation of some "reality," adds value by allowing humans to deal with that "reality." The very act of storing, processing, and communicating 0s and 1s has no value separate from representing that "reality" accurately. Computing places an extremely demanding burden on system developers and operators to portray "reality" accurately by way of coded 0s and 1s. Software, the coded representation of a logical sequence of actions manipulating the coded "reality," is also expressed in 0s and 1s. To define a logical sequence of steps and reduce them to computer-understandable 0s and 1s requires the translation of human mental and perhaps physical actions into coded 0s and 1s (i.e., program instructions). This must be done to such a degree of accuracy that the coded 0s and 1s can be trusted to carry out their function with a high degree of consistency. Such software, when trusted, is said to possess integrity. Executive management of IT needs to be concerned with doing everything possible to construct software and systems with such integrity that they never compromise the trust placed in their representations of "reality."

The Y2K problem has compromised the trust that we humans can continue to place in certain "realities." Because of errors in the 0 and 1 representations of dates, certain outputs from logical sequences of steps (i.e., the software) no longer possessed integrity and systems lost our confidence. Without human confidence, most computing provides no value added. In fact, a devaluation may occur.

The Y2K problem has demonstrated the absolute necessity for managing IT in a manner commensurate with its great demands for precision and the great promise of added value it offers to organizations.

The next chapter catalogs some of the lessons being learned from the Y2K experience as it unfolds.

4

LESSONS BEING LEARNED FROM THE Y2K EXPERIENCE

A PROPHET REVISITED: ROBERT TOWNSEND

In 1988, an American business classic, *Further Up the Organization,* by Robert Townsend was revised and published 18 years after it first appeared as *Up the Organization.* Townsend is probably best known for engineering the turnaround of the Avis Corporation in the 1960s. Before that he was an executive at American Express. Of that experience he has written, "During these years [1948 to 1962] the company was rich enough to do—and did— almost everything wrong. In that near-perfect learning environment I formed the valuable habit of observing what action was taken, considering the opposite course, and then working back, when necessary, to what really made sense."

Using that same strategy, executives of today need to work backward from the way IT has been managed during the last 30 years and start to formulate effective strategies for directing this "new" technology. Before initiating this formulation by developing a list of lessons being learned in the aftermath of Y2K, it will serve our purpose to see what Townsend had to say about "computers and their priests." His words will appear in quotes, my comments in italics. Let's see if his comments on computers were accurate as a predictor of conditions that have resulted in the difficulties we are all now experiencing post–year 2000.

"First get it through your head that computers are big, expensive, fast, dumb adding machines—typewriters." *Today computers are smaller—so small we are not sure where they are, still expensive if we honestly consider all related life-cycle costs, and still dumb. They would have continued processing two-digit dates until programmed to do otherwise or they would have stopped.*

"Then realize that most of the computer technicians you're likely to meet or hire are complicators, not simplifiers. They try to make it look tough. Not easy." *Actually, the business of IT is quite complicated, much more so now than in the 1970s or 1980s. But the inherent complexity of the basic technology often has been greatly compounded within a company by a multitude of unwise implementation strategies and decisions that have led to unnecessary incompatibilities between and among systems.*

"They're building a mystique, a priesthood, their own mumbo-jumbo ritual to keep you from knowing what they—and you—are doing." *Yes, IT people did what lawyers, doctors, accountants, and engineers have done— they have created their own language to use when communicating about their technology. There are, however, a class of IT professionals who specialize in communicating with nontechnical persons. This type of systems analyst needs to be involved in all attempts to translate business requirements into technical language and vice versa. They are the simplifiers.*

"Here are some rules of thumb:

"1. At this state of the art, keep decisions on computers at the highest level. Make sure the climate is ruthlessly hard-nosed about the practicality of every system, every program, and every report. 'What are you going to do with that report?' 'What would you do if you didn't have it?' Otherwise your programmers will be writing their doctoral papers on your machine, and your managers will be drowning in ho-hum reports they've been conned into asking for and are ashamed to admit are of no value." *In addition to doctoral papers, in today's corporation of knowledge workers there will be a lot of net surfing—surfing for information to give your corporation a competitive advantage and surfing for AAA trip guides, recipes, day trading, and to direct resume submittals.*

"2. Make sure your present report system is reasonably clean and effective before you automate. Otherwise your new computer will just speed up the mess." *Who would have thought when this was originally written that some day companies would go back to nonautomated record keeping because of a two-digit date problem? Or try to go back. The very nature of some of today's just-in-time processing systems makes going back, while maintaining any sem-*

blance of efficiency, all but impossible. These systems never had a manual predecessor. They are the products of technological capabilities lashed together into systems that have no previous manual origins. As has become evident, such systems have no effective fallback manual position because their very design was based on emerging capabilities of automation with little or no thought to any limitations that may have accompanied such designs.

"3. Rather than build your own EDP [electronic data processing] staff, hire a small independent software company to come in, plan your computer system, and then get out. Make sure they plan every detail in advance and let them know you expect them to meet every dollar and time target. Systems are like roads. Very expensive. And no good building them until you know exactly where they're going to wind up." *This statement was originally made before the heyday of systems and software methodologies. It was the early 1970s, before the "structured" (i.e., engineering approaches) revolution in development process steps were defined and the late 1970s before the first round of refinements emerged. All were in response to what had become the pressing need to get "discipline" into the business of building computer systems and software. The question for contemporary executives to ponder is: Why have these disciplined approaches not been applied more rigorously? The suggested answer is that executives have not insisted that IT be managed with the same degree of discipline as other facets of the business. Little will change until this shortcoming is corrected.*

"4. Before you hire a computer specialist, make it a condition that he spend some time in the factory and then sell your shoes to the customer. A month the first year, two weeks a year thereafter. This indignity will separate those who want to use their skills to help your company from those who just want to build their know-how on your payroll." *This issue is more critical now than ever before. IT has become extremely specialized. Multiple "priesthoods" now exist not only around the technology in general but in many specific subsets representing languages, database methods, vendor lines, software packages, and so on. Many IT professionals, perhaps the majority, are hired only for one technical specialty, and they essentially perform the same specialty task for many employers regardless of the line of business. There are alternatives, however. On one hand, a corporation can hire skilled practitioners of an element of the total package of mumbo-jumbo but with no appreciable sense of the business for which they are applying their skill. On the other hand, a company can opt to provide technical practitioners with "positions" within the business with the intent of growing the people into a busi-*

ness asset. This will appeal to many IT professionals, since everyone needs a purpose beyond a paycheck—a sense of stability in their lives.

"5. No matter what the experts say, never, never automate a manual function without a long enough period of dual operation. And don't stop the manual system until the non-experts in the organization think that automation is working. I've never known a company seriously injured by automating too slowly, but there are some classic cases of companies bankrupted by computerizing prematurely." *As previously mentioned, systems have been built, and will continue to be built, that have no manual predecessor system to compare against while running parallel. These systems are creations of the technology that were not possible before the technology. All web-based systems are of this type. The alternative to parallel operations is the deliberate and carefully managed use of pilot projects and simulations. Phased implementations, where risk is continually assessed, can serve the purpose of parallel periods of operation. With either approach, parallel running with the predecessor manual system or pilot projects and simulations, executives cannot prematurely force the fielding of systems without assuming great risk. Automation projects driven by all the normal business interests (i.e., short-term revenues, profits, markets, sales, etc.) must be balanced by an active risk management program, especially if there is no manual system to fall back on.*

Little of this advice, of course, will matter to those caught in the fever of new technologies where success is measured by the amount of capital that can be raised through initial stock offerings and not by generating business revenues.

LESSONS BEING LEARNED

It is hoped that the following lessons will be learned as a result of the Y2K experience. Residual problems will impact different systems at different times over several months and so it is difficult to know just when the "aftermath" will begin and end for any given company, agency, nation, or individual. The executive lessons that are going to be learned do not focus at the technical levels of trying to get certain equipment and software to interface successfully so that business can approach normalcy again. No, the important lessons to be learned will change perceptions of IT, how IT must be managed and controlled in the future, and the role that business executives will have to play for these changes to take place. Having just experienced a "significant emotional event," executives and managers will be motivated to seek new "truths" regarding IT and its application to their business. For many, the insights gained because of the year 2000 experience will seem obvious in retrospect. At the same time, they should wonder how they could have expected a technology to manage itself when other technologies must submit to discipline and process.

CRITICALITY OF INFORMATION AND IT SYSTEMS FINALLY RECOGNIZED

The critical nature of information and the systems that deliver it will constitute one of the post–year 2000 insights that, although in retrospect seeming so obvious, will have many managers and executives scrambling for cover. If, the discussion will go, information and IT systems were so critical, how could this have happened? Blame will be leveled at the IT executives, of course, but that will not absolve the directors and officers of their responsibility. The facts, for those dealing in facts, simply will indicate that with few exceptions, information and information technology systems were not managed with the same degree of discipline and scrutiny as were other facets of the business. Information was not viewed as having the same value as the traditional resources of people, money, and materials. Information was viewed not as a corporate asset with serious strategic value but as a by-product, an after-the-fact reporting of past events. For our purposes, information includes strategic decision-making input data as well as the digital signals in a manufacturing control unit to open or close a valve. Some people may recognize that even though untold billions of dollars are spent annually on information processing, very few information products actually are used by executives in making most corporate strategic decisions. Robert Townsend was right: Many executives may be embarrassed in defending how IT dollars actually have been spent.

Acknowledging, even belatedly, that information and their systems are valuable will impart that same value onto the software and processing systems used to manipulate the now-valuable resource of information.

Then will come the realization that computers, software, processing systems, and the methods by which they are developed, acquired, and operated also need executive attention.

THREE IMPORTANT ROLES FOR EXECUTIVES

But what does it mean to say that executives need to become involved in the management of software and systems? It means that executives must insert themselves into a number of *roles* that generally have gone unfilled during most of the short history of IT.

The first and most critical role is that of a business leader using technologies to accomplish goals and objectives that have been carefully thought out so that the uses of IT can be clearly defined and not vaguely implied. Executives who can provide this kind of leadership need to understand the limitations of IT as well as its capabilities, and they will not let themselves become overly enamored with new and untried applications of IT. They will ensure that new applications are treated initially as experiments and kept small in scale. They will require the performance of full feasibility studies.

A second role places the executive in the position of balancing priorities between IT and non-IT activities and among various IT initiatives. Only the executive is equipped to know the big picture and not allow an imbalance to be created between and among projects. Often, in the past, priority wars developed between business units, each with its own pet IT projects. Without executive "balancing," the IT group cannot deal with such situations and may become too timid for the company's own good.

Recognizing that the methods used to develop and operate computer software and support systems are important due to their critical relationship to the integrity of business information and processes, the executive assumes the role of "enforcer." Only the executive can play this role because only the executive has the overall authority to make things happen and operates from a vantage point that allows all perspectives and issues to be aired and resolved.

Enforcement of metrics, standard development methods, and other best-practice consistency across the organization will constitute the giant leap that is most significant for the eventual improvement of IT and will bring about the engineered stability needed for systems to be trusted again. Without enforcement of methods and best practices, nothing will change since the development steps by which systems are built will be different each time, no consistent approach will be documented, and the organization will be open to "reasonableness" attacks from all directions.

IMPORTANCE OF METRICS

Central to the issues of best practices and the standardization on a systems development process is the previously discussed topic of metrics and measurements. For some executives, the shock of learning late in 1999 that systems, heretofore reported on target for the year 2000 compliance deadline, would not make it was a rude wake-up call. If these executives had been listening and watching their organizations, this was not the first time that IT had been late in delivering what had been promised. The statistics, gathered over the last 20 years, show a consistent track record of at least 25 percent of all software projects being canceled, 15 percent delivered behind schedule, with the resulting systems still having on average 75 defects for every ten thousand lines of tested code. And of these systems delivered, only 20 percent are considered an unqualified success by their users. (See Exhibit 1.2.)

Short of out-and-out lying by subordinates, however, executives can blame the inability to get straight answers about the progress of any IT project only on their own failure to establish and live by meaningful IT metrics whereby true progress and other significant aspects of a project's status can be measured. Again, it comes down to not managing IT with the same degree of discipline that other facets of the business have to endure. Metrics, like system development process methods and best practices, need to settle around a core of discrete product and process measures that can be used not only to report project status but, over time, to make calculated process improvements as part of quality management efforts. Appendix A provides a comprehensive catalog of metrics that a well-administered IT organization should be required to keep. This requirement also would extend to decentralized business units possessing their own IT group or support contractors.

RISK MANAGEMENT IS NEEDED WITH ALL IT UNDERTAKINGS

Historically, the issue of IT-related risk has been associated with the topics of security, privacy and fraud, and systems abuse. These topics, however, are a subset of the larger risk management picture dealing with the continuous assessment, for risk, of all aspects of IT and of projects under development for the corporation. For risk management to be effective, it must be directed from the top of the organization with strategic impact evaluations of identified risks being conducted at the top. Risk management and business opportunity analyses are essential job functions of executives. Both types of analysis require their unique perspective to ensure that all pertinent issues and viewpoints are being considered and evaluated.

Senior executives must proactively inquire about risks to the business posed by the use of technology as well as opportunities that the uses of IT afford. While numerous aspects of technology need to be analyzed for individual risk, the accumulation of these risks and their effect on the corporation as a whole must be considered. Information technology has become essential to many fundamental business activities. Any failure of IT results in a domino effect that can be felt throughout the company and in many cases up and down the business partner supply chain. This is especially true with any kind of just-in-time processing or delivery system. Anyone's failure becomes everyone's failure. This relatively new risk scenario requires continuous monitoring so that the totality of the process, across companies, is not adversely affected.

A number of risks uniquely threaten the successful use of IT within a corporation. Those that require executive attention include:

- The possibility of failure of an underlying technology
- The likelihood of support vendor failure
- The probability that IT technical employees can support a project's technology
- The likelihood of losing competitive advantage due to project delays
- The risk of creeping requirements
- The risks posed by emerging liability challenges
- The risks based on meaningless warranties
- The likelihood of new laws and regulations governing IT
- The continuing risk of IT project delays, abandonment, and marginal success rates

The following elements of risk associated with any IT project can be monitored using Appendix C.

Failure of an Underlying Technology

This risk deals not so much with an outright meltdown of a technology but with the gradual erosion of the performance characteristics of particular product manifestations of a technology that over time does not live up to expectations. This risk can affect an IT project adversely because two things happen as expectations are changed. First, the original system's concept will alter as the realization of technological shortcomings force a reexamination of what can be attained—this brings about a change in the requirements as finally implemented. Second, if the technology's promise is too seriously missed, the whole project is likely to be scrapped until a proven technical product can be located. When this occurs, project momentum is often lost and the original system's concept may be overtaken by events.

If the failure of an underlying technology is not discovered until late in a project's development cycle, the adverse impacts may be very severe as the future of the business may have been depending on this particular technology and its implementation. The predicted future of an underlying technology needs to be monitored carefully so that early warnings of problems are discovered in time to adjust product or project plans.

Likelihood of Support Vendor Failure

New underlying technology (i.e., hardware devices, components, and support software) often are exploited by start-up companies comprised of talented engineers, entrepreneurs, and venture capitalists. Early sales are imperative for the future viability of such start-ups. To achieve such sales, companies often employ, at very lucrative commission rates, professional IT sales personnel noted for their success at delivering high-volume orders. They are motivated to make sales and may have little regard for the actual performance of the product, the software, the service, or for after-sales service. In fact, in many start-up companies that are striving to be one of the first to market with an implementation of a new technology, the product may still be a prototype, and after-sales service does not exist beyond a phone call to the "creator" of the product. These are facts of life in the rapidly expanding world of IT. *Caveat emptor* is alive and well when dealing with technology start-ups. The degree of corporate stability and solvency that executives have come to expect of their other business partners may not exist, and this poses special risks to a corporation's foray into any new technology thought to be fundamental to a new business initiative.

IT companies, especially those associated with cutting edge technologies and their implementations, are extremely volatile and susceptible to bankruptcies and takeovers. This area of risk also calls for special monitoring to preclude any surprises as a project progresses along its life cycle.

Likelihood That Employee Marketplace Can Support the Technology

This area of risk is extremely important and difficult to assess. In 1999, the U.S. Commerce Department's Office of Technology Policy estimated that there will be a need for approximately 1.3 million new computer engineers, programmers, and systems analysts over the next decade. At the same time, the Department of Education reports a decline of 40 percent in computer science graduates from 1986 to 1994. If the United States cannot fill this need for IT workers, U.S. innovation, competitiveness, productivity, and economic growth could be undermined.

The problem of skilled personnel shortfalls have plagued IT from the beginning. All new technology proposals need to be tempered by this reality and human resources plans put into place that will address the problem and lessen its impact.

The probability that a specific corporate IT initiative could be affected adversely by a shortage of skilled workers is a function of many factors, including:

- Popularity of the underlying technology or products, is IT seen to be in the mainstream by prospective employees
- Estimated local population of people trained and skilled in the technology or product
- Ability to meet salary requirements of skilled personnel
- Creativity of corporate compensation packages—nonmonetary items
- Ability to create special job or skill compensation packages
- Willingness to offer contracts to critical personnel to better ensure their longevity on a project

- Willingness to subsidize education of IT employees
- Reputation of the corporation as a place to work

Many of the conditions of employment needed to build and maintain a competent and reasonably loyal IT workforce may seem, to non-IT employees, to create a special group—an elite class of employees. The more esoteric the chosen technology, the more elite becomes the IT workforce required to support it. This, of course, can lead to problems not worth the advantage gained by adopting an esoteric technology. It can lead to situations where the company can be held hostage by the only people who understand how the company, with its cutting-edge system, works. Executives must judge carefully if they want to give that kind of power to their technicians. Note that contracting out does not necessarily solve this problem; it just moves the point of risk further from direct control.

Likelihood of Losing Competitive Advantage Due to Project Delay

The difficulty with assessing this type of risk is in attempting to correlate a perceived window of competitive opportunity with the actual, not scheduled, progress being made on an IT project to capitalize on that opportunity. A project of this nature, even while rushed, must be under tight project management control with effective metrics being captured and reported honestly. The first reaction of many IT people would be to "cut corners" with such initiatives to get it done quickly. Some in the IT group will view this type of initiative as a fast track to promotion and influence within the corporation. They will be responding to what they have seen work for others under similar circumstances regardless of what was delivered.

Executives must insist that shortcuts to building a quality and reputation-enhancing system not be taken. They, above all others, must require that appropriate development methods and best practices be followed or else the company may unwisely seize the opportunity from a competitor but do so with a half-baked system that will eventually do more harm than good to the corporate reputation. While the company is backtracking and attempting to recover, the competitor is capitalizing on the mistakes and bad press and taking control of the market.

A final word of caution: Without the senior executive championing a best-practices and sound development approach for challenges such as this, the chief information technologist stands little chance of overcoming the pressures from other executives to get it done quickly, even at the expense of ending up with a supportable and stable system.

Risk of Creeping Requirements

One of the most frequent complaints from IT professionals while attempting to construct an automated system, is that customers/clients/users keep changing the requirements—they do not know what they want. To a limited degree, certain tools and techniques can be used during the early development phases of a system to provide a certain flexibility in dealing with changing requirements. But often the complaint has merit: Customers/clients/users do not know what is needed. This represents one of the greatest risks to a project's success. It has long been known that the most important phase of systems development is the requirements definition phase. Without a clearly documented set of business requirements, which function like blueprints, the subsequent phases of development will likely be a waste. A wonderfully engineered system may result but it is not what was needed and it did not solve the problem or capitalize on the opportunity. As shown in Exhibit 1.2, this is why only 20 percent of systems seem to satisfy a user's working requirement.

The risk of incomplete requirements can be greatly reduced through the adoption and enforcement of a systems development process or methodology. Inherent within such methodologies is the commitment of time sufficient to define adequately the business requirement and to conduct successive reviews to confirm those requirements before actual systems design and programming begins. The *systems development framework* provided as Appendix B follows this approach and should be referred to to ensure that system-related requirements such as security, internal controls, and quality issues are specified before system design and programming begin.

Creeping requirements are a risk when a disciplined requirements definition and confirmation period is not enforced. The vagueness of system goals and objectives are unclear, leading to additional requirements as system and software features are added. No baseline of requirements stabilizes, so systems design and programming cannot proceed. Each time additional requirements creep into the statement of specifications, systems development should pause, reevaluate the design in light of the "new" requirement, reconcile any design inconsistencies, conduct quality assurance reviews, and then proceed with development. If requirements creep in too often, these steps are not likely to be performed with any consistency and the project staff simply will try to fold the new requirement into the development as best they can. Each time a requirement creeps into a system already under development, either the time to completion must be lengthened or the project assumes the risk of modifying a design and program code without the benefit of a thorough impact analysis. Much is sacrificed when system requirements are not locked down at least until a system satisfying the initial requirements is completed.

Risks Posed by Emerging Liability Challenge

Liability challenge, an area of emerging risk, will require concentrated executive attention for the foreseeable future as Y2K litigation rewrites the legal landscape for IT software developers, service providers, value-added resellers, system integrators, and consultants. Likely also to be further defined will be the due diligence responsibilities of accounting, consulting, and legal firms when participating as advisors to mergers and acquisitions.

Managing this area of risk will require the continuous involvement of the corporate legal staff to closely monitor changing developments as software liability cases unfold over the next several years. Regardless of specific liability limitations that now pertain to Y2K litigation, the type of cases now being crafted by lawyers for such litigation will herald the future for software and systems litigation in the 21st century. Corporate legal staffs need to follow developments in the following areas.

Product Liability Claims. Opposing lawyers will collect product information including technical documentation, manuals, advertising materials, bug notifications concerning the product, and internal e-mail postings concerning the product while in development. They will try to establish early corporate knowledge of product malfunctions that may or may not have been corrected before release for sale. Intentions of fixing malfunctions in a next release may not stand up as a defense, depending on severity and the impact on customers.

Breach of Contract. This is the first avenue of litigation in cases where written contracts and implied warranties come into conflict with performance of the system. This is the area where the concept of duty of the "expert" to the "nonexpert" may be tested, regardless of countercharges of contributory negligence.

Fraud and Misrepresentation. Lawyers in discovery will uncover exaggerated product claims, hyped advertising, overoptimistic development schedules, evidence of shortcuts and deviations that were taken from best practices, and employees willing to testify about how warnings were not heeded. Outsourcing firms and consultants may be particularly vulnerable if their advertising claims turn out to be false.

Insurance Claims. Even though most state insurance commissioners ruled that Y2K could be excluded from coverage, this is not true for future claims against *error and omissions* coverage. Exclusions pertain only to Y2K problems. Look for insurance companies to become much more inquisitive about software and systems development practices before continuing to offer future coverage and in determining premiums.

Officers' and Directors' Liability. For future software and system failures, and based on Y2K case precedence, lawyers will want to know when senior management was first informed of a potential problem (i.e., the one for which the company is being sued) and what they did about it. Counsel will argue that such notification started a clock running during which time directors and officers were to have exercised "reasonable care" in the performance of their fiduciary responsibility. Under such circumstances, testimony from employees and copies of warning memoranda will be damaging. The presence of warning memorandum may indicate a project out of control and intimate negligence. Destruction of warning memorandum would indicate a cover-up and may constitute a crime in itself.

Some will argue that as soon as the first director or officer is held liable, all the rest of corporate America will simply isolate themselves from such situations. Such a strategy, however, could backfire, resulting in charges of negligence in the course of executing fiduciary responsibilities.

There are serious management implications associated with each of these scenarios. Simply blaming IT employees for defective software will not stand up in court. In most cases, it will be demonstrated that defective software and systems were the result of trade-off decisions concerning management of the IT project in question. Making trade-off decisions among costs, schedules, and systems quality requires at least the passive participation of senior executives and cannot be relegated to subordinate employees without incurring even greater personal risk. Chief information officers will be especially vulnerable in the years ahead and in many organizations will be forced to take unpopular positions regarding the quality of IT products and services. Without senior executive support and protection, CIO will continue to stand for Career Is Over.

Risks Based on Meaningless Warranties

For those corporations that are greatly dependent on information technology and on the IT industry for software systems and support, there is an emerging special category of risk. This risk centers on the IT industry's continuing attempt to further limit its liability for defective products. This threat comes as part of a new initiative being spearheaded by the software industry, to be found in the *Uniform Computer Information Transactions Act* (UCITA). The UCITA is a proposed law for applying consistent rules to computer software licenses across all 50 states. The UCITA would amend the Uniform Commercial Code (UCC). As of late 1999, the UCITA would essentially:

1. Give vendors the right to repossess software by disabling it remotely
2. Make the terms of off-the-shelf licenses more enforceable
3. Prevent the transfer of licenses from one party to another without vendor permission
4. Outlaw reverse engineering of software
5. Allow vendors to disclaim warranties
6. Allow vendors to not be held accountable for *known* defects

While the first four provisions may seem onerous to some, they are understandable attempts by an industry, besieged by piracy, to protect its intellectual property and revenue stream. The fifth and sixth provisions, however, are far more troubling from the perspective of an individual or corporate buyer. These provisions would seem to allow vendors to disclaim warranties for defective, buggy, or virus-infested software. The provisions say that software publishers are not liable for the poor quality of their products, according to Watts Humphrey, a fellow at the Software Engineering Institute at Carnegie-Mellon University.

Today, any feature that a vendor demonstrates at a trade show or writes about in a product manual must be a working part of the product. The proposed law would seem to change that.

The UCITA, it is feared, will cause a lowering of standards for software performance and will cost user companies more money because, having reduced faith in warranties, they will have to take extra steps to ensure that the software products work properly before buying them.

Risks of this nature call for executive attention to ensure that corporate interests are represented during all IT procurements. Corporations also must participate when legislative agendas of this nature are being proposed. Do not assume that when people are drafting these laws, they are ensuring balance and watching out for everyone's best interest.

Likelihood of Laws and Regulations Governing IT

Opposite to increased protection for IT vendors may be a demand for regulations and laws to bring IT under control. Much will depend on the final fallout from the Y2K experience. If damage turns out to be significant in regulated industries such as financial services and health care, and industries heavily dependent on contract IT services or third-party software, we may see a rush to regulate IT that supports those industries. At a minimum, such regulation probably will require the validation and verification by an independent third party that IT suppliers, to regulated industries, meet or exceed prescribed best-practice standards and are demonstrating "reasonableness" in the management of their product development or support service.

Also expect to see an increase in demands for privacy legislation affecting computerized record keeping. A model for this type of law would be a revised version of the Federal Privacy Act of 1974 that acknowledges contemporary technology threats. Enacted years ahead of its time, the Privacy Act of 1974 pertained to federal record keeping only and set a standard for required record accuracy before making any determination about an individual citizen. The law prescribed procedures for citizens to gain record access, procedures for contesting record content and accuracy, and procedures for ensuring that corrected record data were passed to other government agencies in possession of the originally inaccurate data. The law also called for possible civil sanctions against the government for making adverse determinations about a citizen based on inaccurate data and allowed criminal penalties for individuals who violated the confidentiality of these record systems.

Continuing Risk of IT Project:
Delay, Abandonment, and Marginal Success Rates

In the post–year 2000 environment, the most serious risks that must be overcome are those associated with continuing to conduct the business of IT in such a fashion that the vast majority of projects are delayed, abandoned, or considered marginal successes. As mentioned earlier:

- 25 percent of all IT projects are abandoned
- At least 15 percent are delayed seven months or more
- 20 percent are considered successes by those using the systems that are finally delivered
- 40 percent are considered to have made marginal improvements
- 40 percent are considered failures

Unless and until this ultimate risk is recognized, accepted as a business fact, and managed from the executive suite, many of the anticipated technology advances of the next decade will not be realized. The difficulties that have just been experienced with the Y2K date computing problem would seem to indicate that IT is rapidly approaching the point where system delivery statistics can only get worse. IT complexities, uncertainties, methodological insufficiencies, skill shortages, and business partner IT problems have reached such crisis proportions that only the most continuous senior executive involvement can effect the changes needed to utilize this technology efficiently. Only with executive leadership can the persistent confusion concerning IT issues be brought under control.

The first steps in controlling this most crucial risk factor is to reassess the role of IT within the business and to determine the extent of the company's dependency on IT and IT workers, suppliers, and business partners who themselves are heavily dependent on IT. The entire spectrum of IT practices and IT relationships must be reevaluated from a weakest-link perspective, and necessary steps must be taken to improve those practices and to work with or replace deficient business partners. In the Y2K aftermath it should be quite clear which suppliers and partners are worth working with and which need to be replaced.

With regard to internal IT project practices, senior executives, like it or not, must take a much more active role in making IT decisions and participate directly in methodology enforcement and project reviews. Joint accountability must become part of the business unit, and IT manager's vocabulary and troubled projects must be discovered early enough for management to take meaningful and effective corrective action.

Depending on the extent of corporate IT dependence and the degree of confidence that now exists in the IT management team, executives may be able to tailor their direct involvement based on a business criticality metric that relates IT projects directly to business importance. It is not advised to tailor executive involvement based solely on a dollar threshold metric since it is difficult to get a clear picture of multiple project interrelatedness using this approach; and it is also too easy for clever technology promoters to package a large, expensive proposition into smaller (i.e., below-the-dollar-threshold) projects and evade executive oversight.

Experience shows that success ratios for IT projects seem to increase significantly when each technology initiative has a business unit sponsor to provide moral support. Even technology improvements that are primarily IT infrastructure-oriented and generally transparent to the business user can benefit from a business unit sponsor equipped to go to bat for the IT group and, if needed, convince other business units of the benefit of the initiative. The business benefit of IT initiatives that originate in the technology group without sponsorship always should be questioned. By constantly linking IT initiatives to business benefit, the executive has changed the backdrop against which many previous technology projects probably were launched. Many factors have made this seemingly obvious approach to judging IT project appropriateness difficult for a number of organizations. Chief among these problems has been a reluctance of senior executives to roll up their sleeves and "work" the technology issues facing their companies. Another reason is that without an agreed-upon vocabulary for determining requirements, no structured method for satisfying those requirements, and no agreed-upon set of metrics to measure progress and performance, there is little for executives and IT managers to discuss constructively. Without realistic expectations, schedules, and budgets, progress reviews of projects become exercises in trying to manage ill-defined perceptions and conflicting impressions of progress based on multiple and conflicting definitions. In other words, IT managers and executives are generally not singing from the same sheet music.

For at least a decade, a major reported goal of CEOs has been to better align the goals of IT and business. The very fact that these two sets of goals are perceived to be out of alignment evidences the problems both groups are having communicating. It should be obvious that IT systems and personnel, computers, and other related assets exist to support the business and not the reverse—and yet many CEOs see lack of mutual alignment as a problem. Is the IT group or the IT support contractor running the corporation? How could that be? It can be true only if a leadership vacuum exists at the top of the company. It can be true only if senior corporate executives, not understanding the critical nature of their IT dependence, have delegated responsibility too low in the organization to effect coordinated, enterprise-wide action. Some people will contend that IT is too complex to be managed from the executive suite. Others will hold that this approach will result in micromanagement and that projects will get even later and more expensive because of it.

This last criticism may be true if senior executives are monitoring the wrong or too many activities and manage against the wrong success criteria. But it is not true if appropriate IT project activities are selected for executive review and if success criteria for an IT undertaking are consistent with the success criteria of the business unit that the project supports. This latter factor alone will ensure the alignment of IT and business goals, while the former will guarantee that IT projects are being managed against a prescribed process for measuring progress. Appendix B presents a model for an appropriate level of executive engagement in IT project and system development management. It outlines a general-purpose systems development process model that includes the critical areas of development and project management activity that need to be reviewed periodically by oversight management. Chapter 5 describes how the model can be used by executives in the post–year 2000 world of IT.

But executive involvement in IT development and project management reviews is not the complete answer to reducing the risk of project delay, abandonment, and marginal success. A senior executive risk management review forum must periodically examine the entire spectrum of risks that may adversely impact IT projects under development and existing systems to determine how related risks can threaten the business as a whole. Again, Appendix C presents worksheets for facilitating such examinations. The objective is to systematically identify, review, and approve all aspects of ongoing IT initiatives based on executive acceptance of reasonable risk. A major consequence of the Y2K experience will be the future requirement to demonstrate that potential risks to a project's success were considered and that a reasonably managed course of IT implementation was undertaken. There will be universal acknowledgment that IT is not magic, that processes need to exist to build quality systems in a cost-efficient manner, and that managing the risks to IT success is a "reasonable" thing to do. Monitoring risk falls into the category of fiduciary responsibility and will be expected of corporate officers and directors.

IMPORTANCE OF DOCUMENTATION IS FINALLY RECOGNIZED

One of the major sources of the Y2K frustration was directly attributable to the lack of accurate and current documentation. As Y2K litigation progresses, the importance of documentation will become even more evident since documentation provides the basis for demonstrating that organizations acted prudently and exercised reasonable care in addressing their responsibilities. Likely, many organizations will not be able to meet this challenge adequately; consequently they will be unable to prove that they exercised due diligence. This fact may well create a standard for future software and system litigation actions and therefore needs to be placed high on the priority list of IT issues demanding executive attention.

Historically, documentation, describing the inner workings of software and systems, has been viewed as a secondary task to getting the code to work and as such was relegated to the project "clean-up" phase to be accomplished before the developers went on to new assignments. This has never worked for a variety of reasons, not the least of which is the fact that systems documentation is boring stuff to generate and maintain and no self-respecting, creative programmer wants to waste time doing it.

Documentation, however, is perhaps the most effective way to judge (as in litigate) the soundness of a system or software development effort. The quality and completeness of documentation reflects the quality and completeness of the software or system it describes and indicates whether management knew enough of what was being designed, programmed, and tested to have been able to exert control over it. Many people will claim that they were in control, but few will be able to prove it. (See Appendix D.) Being unable to demonstrate control over the development process will bring into doubt claims of having acted in a reasonable and prudent manner.

What constitutes comprehensive documentation? There are different requirements for the different phases of systems development. Since documentation can be thought of as the glue holding a system together, what should executives and managers expect to see? First, each phase of the systems development process, has work products, and each product should be documented to the extent needed to be understandable by a reasonably skilled independent analyst. This is important because of staff turnover and the fact that much of the documentation from a development phase actually serves as instructions to another analyst performing tasks in another phase of the development process. Documentation serves to remove ambiguity and present a clear, concise, and accurate description of some part of a system so that someone other than the original creator can understand what was intended and what was built.

By way of comparison, systems and software documentation is analogous to the various trade views or blueprints associated with home construction. Separate blueprints may depict different views of the house's design—floor plans, plumbing, electrical, landscaping. Equally important for a systems or software development effort are the design documents that describe the database, software logic, hardware, network, and general system processing flow documents. Each document serves the same purpose for systems development as blueprints and trade views do for housing construction. Each describes the specific components of the planned automated system in enough detail to satisfy the following objectives:

- Construct and integrate, using hardware and software components, a computer processing system that improves and does not impede the business activities of the organization.

- Construct the system to the level of quality, security, and performance demanded of the business activity.

- Construct the system in a timely fashion while still allowing for thoroughness of testing internally, and externally with affected business partners.

- Allow for the efficient use of technical and human resources during development.
- Deliver a system that can be operated, modified, and maintained within a reasonably accurate cost projection.

Due to the unforgiving nature of computers, a great deal of detailed information is required in the finished documents. Such documentation should adhere to certain standards.* This will minimize ambiguity and guard against development team confusion should it experience turnover during the project's development or during system operation.

Finally, system documentation forms the basis for an enforceable contract and is the starting point for resolving contract disagreements. The bottom line in resolving disputes is the statement of work or the documented system specification that states what was expected of the contractor, what was acceptable to the customer, when it was to be delivered, and at what price.

From an operational perspective, documentation also must serve to facilitate rapid recovery should system downtime be experienced. Rapid recovery is directly dependent on the adequacy of documentation. Without complete, accurate, and current documentation, system failures cannot be traced, diagnosed, analyzed, corrected, and tested. Without usable manuals, listings, diagrams, and the like, the business process stays down and revenue and customers are lost. This is the lesson that Y2K has demonstrated so clearly. In the future, no system or software project can ever be considered finished unless complete and accurate documentation is delivered before the system goes into operation.

Outsourcing or contracting for IT services does nothing to lessen this requirement. In fact, the opposite may be true. Outsourcing may make the documentation issue even more critical. Under an outsource arrangement, a corporation may not have the right or the opportunity to assess the condition of documentation the contractor is using to operate and maintain the systems that support IT processing. Often, documents and procedures are considered to be an outsourcer's proprietary materials. A firm contracts for a service, much like snow removal, and how the contractor ac-

*Documentation Standards are available through American Society for Quality, The National Institute for Science and Technology, U.S. Department of Commerce, or the International Standards Organization.

complishes the task is not your business, so long as the snow gets removed. Unless the contract is specific as to how processing tasks are to be performed, within the constraints of certain standards and including documentation standards, a company may have little to say after the fact. Even being specific provides no guarantees that such documents actually are maintained or properly used. A business must hope for the best, knowing that it is at the mercy of the contractor.

Most contracts with penalty clauses do not adequately protect a company. Carefully check those penalties and compare what is recoverable from the contractor vs. what is at risk. The two probably are not balanced in the least.

A partial solution is to stay clear of standard contract language and negotiate a firm's own penalty clauses—as severe as possible. The very act of negotiation may, in fact, give indicators of the level of confidence the potential contractor has in the quality of not only its documentation and processes but also its services and systems. Within reason, this tactic will work; get too demanding, however, and the contractor may agree to anything to get or keep the business, and then both the firm and the contractor may be hoping for the best.

What constitutes adequate documentation for a system on completion of a development project? What should an outsourcer have in the way of manuals, procedures, and software-related listings and diagrams to guide the processing of the corporation's vital systems and records? Finalized documentation for systems and software should generally include:

- High-level work-flow and information flow charts with detailed narrative statements describing the business system functions.
- Data and database descriptions, formats; software programs that edit, update, manipulate, and otherwise manage the data collection; and instructions for archiving and backing up data.
- Software design documents adhering to any one of several structured notations; logic trees and conditional branching logic; data exchanges between applications both inside and outside the organization.
- Software edit routines for excluding error data and error resolution procedures for correcting erroneous inputs.
- Security access and processing controls to ensure confidentiality and data integrity and system availability.

- Checkpoints where the accuracy of transactions in process are reviewed—interrupt processing and restart procedures.
- Journal logs required for audit purposes.
- Output controls to ensure secure and confidential delivery of information products.
- A complete description of manual processes that accompany the automated system.
- Operating instructions for system users and technical maintenance personnel to include security, audit, and network administrators.
- Configuration information for both software and hardware sufficient to perform systems upgrades and software maintenance.
- Curriculum and instructional materials sufficient to prepare future employees for system operation and maintenance.
- Warranty and maintenance agreements identifying periods of service and response times expected from contractors.
- Up-to-date test plans, test data, and test results.
- Disaster recovery and contingency plans.

This discussion has been at a more detailed level than may seem appropriate for the reader, but the criticality of documentation cannot be overstated and recent year 2000 experiences would seem to support that contention. People cannot manage what they cannot describe, and since it is increasingly unlikely that a single person can understand most systems, the more dependent companies become on the written or otherwise recorded representation of what these systems are doing.

INDEPENDENT VALIDATION, VERIFICATION, AND TESTING PROVIDE ASSURANCES

Prior to the Y2K problem, independent validation, verification, and testing (IVV&T) were activities reserved for the space program and other IT life-critical applications. During government and corporate attempts to resolve the Y2K date problem, many organizations adopted all or parts of IVV&T in order to provide a greater degree of certitude that problems were, in fact, being corrected and that systems would operate properly. Validation is concerned with determining whether a development team has constructed a *correct or proper system* to meet the business requirement. Verification has to do with confirming or substantiating that the processes, techniques, and tools used during construction of the system were properly utilized and that best practices were followed. Testing, of course, is an integral part of the system development process and is variously considered to be a development duty as well as a quality assurance (QA) or quality control activity. Independent testing, regardless of developmental or QA testing, is accomplished both to validate and verify the final readiness of systems and software declared to be complete and available for use or shipment. During an IVV&T period, anomalies and defects are discovered in even well-developed systems.

An IVV&T effort can be structured to have semi-independence by being performed by corporate employees separate from the developers and responsible through a different management path for their findings. Or an IVV&T effort can be contracted out to another company whose allegiance is to its reputation for providing sound evaluations and advice to client executives regarding the readiness of a system or software product.

IVV&T examines system development work products to ascertain whether

- Hardware and software components have been programmed and integrated properly according to best practices of the industry.

- System components deliver the required results—expected of the design to satisfy the business requirement.

- Requirements can be traced through the system documentation to actual executable code somewhere in the software and that they were tested.

The principal method to determine the soundness of a development effort is to observe a close correlation between the project under evaluation and any structured systems development methodology of the last 20 years. Appendix B provides a high-level summary of those actions that commonly need to occur for a development effort to be considered best practice. While the technical nomenclature of a particular methodology may differ, all methodologies are similar in their adoption of traditional engineering principles, used in complex problem solving, and applying them to software and systems development. Essentially, each methodology outlines a method for defining a problem, designing a solution, building the solution, and testing and correcting the final solution until all risks, to everyone, have been reduced to an acceptable level for all concerned.

The Y2K experience has emphasized the importance of identifying IT risks, not only to one's own organization but to all those parties impacted by its products and services. The degree of care that must be taken in developing and delivering those products and services is determined by identified risks and the actions taken to eliminate those risks so that an objective observer (i.e., a jury) can conclude that a firm acted reasonably given what was at stake.

IVV&T is becoming essential for demonstrating that care was taken during the development of an IT product or service because it indicates that a corporation treats the issue of system-related risk seriously and that it believes it is the firm's responsibility to take reasonable actions to reduce or minimize those risks.

Another method for determining the soundness of a development effort is to perform independent system tests and conduct a thorough review of all testing documentation. Historically, system testing activities have been given little attention until the final delivery and acceptance phases of the project. But to be truly effective, testing must be an element of the ongoing QA activity during the process of requirements definition, system design, and programming. During an independent review of a systems development effort, IT managers should be able to demonstrate the following:

- A test effort separate from the development team
- Testing budget and schedule
- Plans outlining what aspects of the system, both automated and manually, are to be tested
- Existence of specific success criteria against which testing results are compared
- Packages of test documentation describing all tests and how they are to be performed—in enough detail that system professionals other than the original tester could run the tests at a later time
- Identified defects, defect resolution procedures, and final test reports
- A database of testing scripts and test metrics for future use and analysis

The criticality of the system being built determines the extent and associated expense of an IVV&T effort. As discussed, risk to the corporation and to customers and business partners will determine the issue of criticality.

For a parking lot permit system, perhaps the quality assurance and test actions of the original programmer may be considered adequate. What is at risk? How might the corporation be liable should the system experience failures or generate bad data? For a financial management support system being integrated with an inventory and reorder system, perhaps a series of peer reviews, code walkthroughs, and comprehensive unit, systems, and integration tests by the integrator may be sufficient. What is at risk? What losses might the corporation incur should there be a systems failure? How might the company be liable should the system fail or generate bad data? Where political fallout, liabilities, or career security loom large, an independent IVV&T may comfort those at risk. Finally, for an air traffic control application, nothing but a completely independent review by a qualified external testing group could be considered sufficient. What is at risk and the associated liabilities are clear to all.

IVV&T must be considered one of the principle ways that organizations can manage risk. This practice has the power to accomplish a great many things for the corporate executive worried about IT issues following the Y2K experience. First, IVV&T, as a functioning element of system development activities, provides assurances to others that a corporation is serious about its responsibility to develop and field quality software and systems. Second, IVV&T actually does improve the quality of systems. Overall costs go down because fewer defects will get released and then have to be fixed retroactively at great expense and at a loss of reputation. Third, IVV&T, in the aftermath of Y2K, will be seen as necessary by competitors as well, so no one will suffer a disadvantage by concentrating on quality of systems and comprehensive risk-reduction techniques. Before the Y2K experience, many software developers would argue that too much QA and too much testing would prevent their hitting the marketing window of opportunity. After Y2K, "enlightened" software developers will understand the shift to quality and will market how QA-sensitive they are and how their products have been verified and tested independently before release.

Everyone will suddenly remember the total quality management (TQM) program of the late 1980s, brush it off, and initiate a revitalized quality improvement initiative.

Fourth, IVV&T should become a hot topic with insurance companies, which will become much more inquisitive concerning the methods and techniques employed by firms while building products or when delivering IT services. For products, this means adherence to an SDP methodology and, when there is sufficient risk, the use of IVV&T techniques to improve the quality of software and systems delivered. For IT service companies and outsources, insurance carriers will be interested in project management techniques and procedures and whether projects are managed according to industry best practices, such as utilizing IVV&T contractors to review and consult on high-risk tasks before delivery to customers.

Finally, the increased use of IVV&T techniques sends a clear signal to in-house IT staff and support contractors that the days of undisciplined development are over and that there now is a way to check on them.

EXECUTIVE-LEVEL DENIABILITY WILL BE HARDER TO CLAIM IN THE FUTURE

The Y2K experience is clearly establishing that corporate executives are responsible for what occurs, or what does not occur, in their organizations. With the exception of a few environmental impact or medical product and implant cases, nothing has threatened the personal tranquility of executives like Y2K and its aftermath. The publicity surrounding the issue and the broad spectrum of system failures has made it difficult for executives to claim any sort of plausible deniability as a defense against lawsuits aimed at them as officers and directors. This fact will change forever the relationship between corporate executives and the uses of IT within and in the name of the corporation. Materiality of corporate IT decisions is being established now, and the implications should be interesting. It will be far more difficult for executives to claim they did not know what was going on with regard to IT because its impact is now so great in most corporations, that to claim ignorance is to admit to incompetence or worse. If plausible deniability is gone, then the most important lesson to be learned from the Y2K experience is to manage IT as any other critical corporate asset would be managed and take control of the technology.

DARE TO MANAGE IT, OR LOSE CONTROL OVER THE BUSINESS

In less than 30 years, business has evolved from the era of accounting machines, typewriters, and telephones to a world of computers, software, and Internet communications. The skills to conduct business support activities have evolved from typing, filing, calculating machine operation, shorthand, telephone operation, and graphic artists to the expectation that employees will master the multitude of functions available in the latest releases of office management software in addition, in most cases, to doing the primary job for which they were hired. Such software, of course, has made it easy to pursue the cost-reduction strategy of layoffs and forced early retirements.

Outside the office environment, manufacturing processes have been computerized and the flow of raw materials through manufacturing to final retail sale and delivery to the customer are controlled by just-in-time systems for the express purpose of keeping inventories at a minimum and reducing costs.

The uses of automation to implement these cost-reduction strategies has been highly successful by most economic measures. But such success has come at a price—a price that was not clearly recognized until the Y2K experience began to unfold. The price is one of dependency. With this dependency comes all the costs and issues associated with trying to conduct business using a technology not under our control. It is not under control of our business partners, either, and it is not under the control of the information technology industry—although a business may, in fact, be under the control of an IT vendor or service provider company. Some executives, for example, are just now becoming aware how great these dependencies have become as they seek to explain to the board of directors and shareholders how a first-, second-, or third-tier component supplier's computer failure has adversely affected the projected revenues and profits for the corporation. What is even harder to explain is how an obscure software vendor's failure to get its product Y2K compliant could have started a sequence of dominos falling in such a way as to adversely affect the corporation. Did the company not have a backup plan? When did the potential failure become known? Why did the company not stockpile parts? It may be hard for some members of the board or for shareholders to comprehend how such a "fragile" system of systems could come to control the corporation. Who is responsible? Why were such dependencies allowed to develop? Who approved this way of doing business? And, finally, the only constructive question: How do we manage these kinds of dependencies in the future?

In Chapter 5, IT management and the new role of proactive executive involvement is discussed. To that end, it is important to establish the readiness of the business to change the way IT has been managed and the willingness of executives to guide that change and insist that future IT be managed carefully and controlled tightly.

In establishing the degree of dedication needed to make such changes, consider the company's answers to the following questions:

Regarding the Year 2000 Experience

Question 1. Is the corporation currently suffering any ill effects from a Y2K–related incident? Do you even know?

Question 2. Is the incident associated with systems or software that was claimed compliant by managers, suppliers, or business partners?

Question 3. Are you comfortable with the explanation you have been given—does it pass the "reasonableness" test?

Question 4. Are you comfortable with the idea of presenting the explanations you have been given to the board of directors, stockholders, or government regulators?

Question 5. Have you been sued for Y2K–related problems?

Question 6. Is the corporation considering a lawsuit against any other party?

Regarding Overall Corporate IT Track Record

Question 1. Do you feel that you are in control of information technology and the impact it is having on the company?

Question 2. Is the corporation getting its IT dollars worth, or is it just one expense after another?

Question 3. Are promised projects delivered on time and within budget?

Question 4. Do IT systems work and give the expected results?

Question 5. Are the systems easily operated and maintained? Can you even tell?

Question 6. Are you comfortable or uncomfortable about the company's degree of dependence on external IT providers?

5

IMPROVING IT MANAGEMENT IN THE TWENTY-FIRST CENTURY

During the past decade, the role of IT has shifted from its traditional back-office functional focus toward one that pervades and influences the fundamental core business activities of the corporation, government agency, or nonprofit organization. IT not only affects how the business must be managed but greatly influences the way in which resources are spent. According to *Fortune* magazine, during calendar year 2000 total spending by business on IT will surpass total spending on other capital goods.

To be sure, in recent years the executive has been inundated with advice and theories regarding the promise of IT and how IT could be used, indeed must be used, for the business to compete and thrive. Every step of the journey toward the ultimate application of IT comes with ever increasing rapidity, and executives constantly are cautioned to be vigilant against falling behind their competitors. Always capabilities and promises, never a mention of limitations and "blown" project estimates. Always strategic uses of IT to dominate a market, never a caution to check on a vendor's dedication to testing and complete documentation. Always articles about exploiting the next technological breakthrough, never a warning that the IT staff is becoming overwhelmed by complexity and how to tell if they are about to walk out the door.

Then executive America learned about the Y2K problem and how long-term inattention and procrastination coupled with decades of undisciplined systems management could threaten their very existence. It is said that "the devil is in the details," and the Y2K experience proved the statement to be true.

But how to proceed to make necessary changes? If "the details" were not being attended to with regard to a two-digit date field, what other details are not being attended to right now, today, tomorrow, and next year? If this kind of operational mess and unnecessary expense are the result of a previous lack of IT management, what can be done to remedy the situation for the future?

First, executives must recognize that the challenge of bringing discipline to the use of IT, like it or not and for the foreseeable future, must be their job. As previously stated, for many corporations, information technology investments now exceed all other forms of capital investment, while information itself is coming to be seen not only as the "glue" that holds an enterprise together but as central to the knowledge base that gives a competitive advantage. In short, management decisions concerning information and the technology that captures, processes, and delivers it are far too important to delegate too far from the executive suite. And until confidence returns that IT is being capably managed, it will need intimate oversight. This is not because everyone else is incompetent or ignorant or stupid, but because for too long, critical IT decisions have been made without the appropriate level of involvement by those executives who legally run the corporation and are answerable to many stakeholders and interest groups for decisions that affect all aspects of the business.

According to Peter Drucker in his latest book, *Management Challenges for the 21st Century,* change has become the norm and the job of executives is to lead change. "Being a change leader requires the willingness and ability to change what is already being done just as much as the ability to do new and different things. It requires policies and practices that make the present create the future."* In the case of the IT problem, change leaders must change what is already being done (i.e., how IT is currently managed) if they hope to be able to do *new and different things.* This is because the new and different things will almost certainly find their origins in IT and in ways to exploit it.

Again, according to Drucker, "Whatever an enterprise does, both internally and externally, needs to be improved systematically and continually: the product or service, the production processes, marketing, technology, the training and development of people, and the use of information." I would

*From Drucker, Peter F. 1999. *Management Challenges for the 21st Century.* New York: HarperBusiness.

include the processes used in the management of information technology and the methods by which information processing systems are built.

So how should executives act as change leaders seeking to take control of their IT future? What is required? What must they undertake to change the future tapestry of IT management?

ESTABLISH EXECUTIVE OWNERSHIP OF INFORMATION AND IT PROJECTS

Pre–Year 2000 Thinking

The prevailing view of information technology, and the uses to which it has been applied, traditionally has been one of sophisticated clerical activity. Except for applications of science and research, until recently most uses of IT have dealt with record keeping and report generation. This early perception of computers and their uses as principally providing administrative support did not command a deep involvement of senior management except to approve budgets for systems that were conventionally also seen as status symbols. Under these conditions, the gradual creep of business dependencies on IT was not recognized. In many cases, not until organizations had to deal with the Y2K problem and were forced to prioritize, due to time constraints, the systems requiring corrective action was the nature of this dependency recognized. Until then, and because of the inadequate view of systems as merely administrative and therefore clerical in nature, many non-IT managers and executives believed that business processes could be accomplished manually if need be. This unrealistic belief was carried forward into the development of recent Y2K contingency plans, as if, for example, a practical solution to an automated payment system failure was to write millions of checks by hand. Or that the volumes of daily purchase transaction processing through a web site could be done manually without a very severe loss of revenues and customers.

In the aftermath of Y2K, the impact of this mistaken belief is proving to be the undoing of some businesses. Years of creeping dependency and inadequate IT management have put main-line business processes at risk and will continue to do so unless executive managers, as change leaders, take ownership of IT and its future applications and control the risks inherent in its use.

Post–Year 2000 Thinking and Practice

Contemporary computing decisions must anticipate the collective needs of all organizational components and their requirement to interoperate. This requirement will affect a company internally as information comes to be viewed more as a source of intelligence to be analyzed and less mere clerical recordings of sales and inventories. Collective information needs and therefore system design and implementation decisions will likely extend outside the corporation to business partners and suppliers with whom the company must coordinate complex just-in-time schedules.

This post–year 2000 reality means that information systems and the uses of IT need to be more highly standardized so that future systems communicating up and down a supply chain are not plagued with interoperability problems that can overwhelm the ability to coordinate rapid system changes necessitated by fluctuating business needs.

Corporations must design their own intrasystem communications around corporate standards and then present a uniform IT environment for dealings with the outside world. A uniform environment managed from the executive suite treats information and IT as a valued asset and is risk-sensitive in making IT decisions and in setting strategy.

Recommendation 1: Establish or reinvigorate the executive IT management committee chaired by the chief executive officer. Depending on how troubled the IT aspects of the organization appear to be, this committee must dedicate a significant amount of time to getting things under control. If serious Y2K problems are being experienced or if other IT projects are in difficulty, this committee may need to meet at least weekly for the foreseeable future. In addition to the CEO, membership should be comprised of the CIO, the business unit directors, the CFO, general counsel, and contracting. If the company offers IT products and services for sale, the director of marketing and sales also must be on the committee.

Recommendation 2: Based on current inventory data, ensure that all automated businesses systems, software application systems, and processing support systems are the direct responsibility of some member of the executive IT management committee. This means that all systems-related prioritization and conflict resolution can take place in the committee. It is imperative that IT be viewed as a collective asset to be utilized by the business as a whole and not islands of computing in competition with each other. Even if the corporate management philosophy is based on internal business unit competition, care must be taken not to let such competition result in non-compatible IT systems and databases sprouting up throughout the corporation. That would only compound the serious problem already existing in many organizations.

DETERMINE APPROPRIATENESS OF IT PROJECTS THROUGH EXPANDED FEASIBILITY ANALYSIS

Pre–Year 2000 Thinking

A common management attitude of many IT-intensive organizations has been that any application of the technology must certainly be good and that the long-term upside always will overcome any short-term difficulty. It has almost become a tenet of faith that new technology is always better than old and must be embraced. The business sponsor for the new technology pushes hard, the technicians push hard, the cost–benefit studies *always* look positive, and few counsel for caution. And yet the track record for delivered IT projects does not impress. As presented previously, some 40 percent of projects fail, another 40 percent are considered marginal, and perhaps 20 percent are acknowledged to be successful from the user's perspective. One possible explanation for the marginal and low user acceptance percentages is that at some level the proposed technology system is not an appropriate use of IT when all the variables necessary for success are considered.

If an IT undertaking was being pursued only for its future potentiality, then it would be planned and developed as a pilot project from which the principal dividend would be knowledge. If, on the other hand, the IT undertaking was to address an operational business problem or seize upon a definable opportunity, then the analysis to determine an appropriate solution should have been more rigorous with an eye to the practical. Of the tools available to make these determinations, the most powerful is the feasibility analysis. But as discussed earlier, feasibility analyses are seldom conducted in their entirety. When conducted, they usually are biased toward the technical and are little concerned with operational aspects. Generally, they portray an incomplete economic picture since all items of expense usually are not considered over the expected life of the system. What executives usually are presented with are analyses conducted by technicians to further advance the company's technical commitments. Business users, and to some extent even internal customers, are not considered to the same degree that technicians factored in their own future prospects by ensuring that they will be working with new technologies.

Post–Year 2000 Thinking and Practice

In the wake of Y2K, the critical eye of practicality will fall on future IT proposals, and the process of feasibility analysis will receive new impetus as the disciplined method for determining what is truly practical. The need to balance the technical aspects of an IT proposal against operational and economic issues finally will be appreciated. To recap briefly the earlier discussion:

• *Technical feasibility* seeks to determine the probability that an IT solution will work and questions whether there is a viable IT-industry support infrastructure to allow the implementation and maintenance of the proposed technology. Is it a tested technology, or will the company be put into guinea pig status by pursuing the proposal? If so, then this status should be consciously chosen and planned for accordingly with expectations kept in line with the risks being assumed.

• *Operational feasibility* concerns itself with whether the IT proposal can be assimilated smoothly into current business processes and what actions must be taken to prepare the workplace to receive the new technology. This analysis must be performed by the operational or business unit directors, not the IT technical staff. Operational feasibility needs to address the elements found to the right side of Exhibit 1.4. Typically, these employee/user activities have not been given proper attention, resulting in the likelihood of unnecessary workplace disruption and eventual adverse customer impact. Operational feasibility also surfaces many more items of expense than the technical study will identify. This increasingly accurate picture of overall costs will result in a more representative and meaningful economic analysis.

• *Economic feasibility* is last in the sequence of studies to prevent choosing an IT proposal based on an incomplete portrayal of total cost of ownership. Too many so-called benefit analyses have painted overly optimistic benefits sides of the equations and woefully inadequate expense sides. The result is that most IT projects are undercapitalized and initiated with completely unrealistic performance expectations. When expectations are unreal, a project is in trouble from day one. This usually results in a series of project compromises that end up satisfying no one while costing a great deal more than anticipated.

Recommendation 3: Establish policy that all IT proposals be subjected to a full feasibility analysis conducted in the sequence of technical, operational, and economic studies. This policy will ensure a standard method for comparing a variety of IT proposals, coming from different organizational components, for overall benefits and impacts on the corporation. The sequence of the three studies will help to ensure that uses of IT will not be overly biased by technical promises but have been balanced by workplace/employee/customer considerations and that realistic overall costs are forcing a well-thought-out statement of benefits covering the life of the system. This policy will result in more realistic expectations on the part of all stakeholders to the proposal and will lessen pressures to compromise on project goals and development discipline in an effort to salvage an ill-defined undertaking.

Recommendation 4: Require that return on investment and cost ownership studies not be substituted for the economic study of the full feasibility analysis. These two popular studies used to determine a cost/benefit profile of an investment in information technology do not necessarily provide the same insights as the cumulative picture provided by a technical, operational, and economic analysis performed in that sequence. Again, experience indicates that most system failures derive from technical infrastructure support difficulties and internal operational integration problems. Until such potential problem areas are given a full measure of attention, the complete extent of potential implementation and maintenance expenses cannot be factored into any form of economic justification.

ESTABLISH EXECUTIVE-LEVEL IT RISK MANAGEMENT REVIEW PROCESS

Pre–Year 2000 Thinking

Risks and risk management, with regard to information technology, generally have been associated with computer security, confidentiality, and perhaps fraud, waste, and system abuse issues. While these are all valid concerns, they need to be addressed within a larger framework. The recent Y2K experience has, directly and indirectly, forced organizations to acknowledge a far broader range of risks than those traditionally recognized. For example, before the Y2K problem, few corporations gave much thought to the technical viability of their supply line of raw materials or component parts. It was pretty much assumed that, short of fraudulent activity or natural disaster, suppliers would make good on their commitments and honor their contracts. Today, it is known that something as seemingly insignificant as the absence of two digits can cause far-reaching problems both up and down a vertical manufacturing line, a manufacturing to retail distribution chain, or a benefits distribution network. The interdependencies among businesses have become much more evident, and prudent future management would seem to require methods to address the inherent risks arising from those interdependencies.

"Acts of God" always have constituted a threat to continued business operation and as such usually have been covered by some form of insurance. After the Y2K, it is likely that insurance companies will be more circumspect when writing coverage with regard to IT-related risks. Probably insurance carriers will become increasingly interested in how IT-intensive businesses manage their IT-related risks and what they do to prevent and/or mitigate the adverse side effects of certain risk scenarios materializing.

Post–Year 2000 Thinking and Practice

Many previously neglected management disciplines need to be applied to the IT industry and by those businesses with significant dependencies on IT. Expanded-focus risk management is one such discipline that, when implemented, needs to be able to identify and monitor risks far beyond the traditional concerns of security and confidentiality and fraud, waste, and system abuse. This new expanded focus on IT risk considers all facets of IT development and project risks and other environmental conditions that can threaten successful implementation of an IT solution. This expanded focus would include any of those areas of risk identified during the feasibility analysis and continue to monitor them for changing conditions.

Appendix C, risk management review models, presents a guide for executive involvement in the management of risk areas associated with corporate uses of IT, suppliers and vendors, and operational factors that can adversely affect the enterprise. Special efforts must be made to identify risks in at least five areas:

1. Breakthrough technologies and new business technologies
2. Software development and systems integration
3. Security, confidentiality, fraud, and system abuse
4. Contractor/supplier dependencies
5. Operations and maintenance for the long term

The models allow for structured monitoring of identified risks so that increasingly appropriate actions can be taken to prevent or minimize threats to IT initiatives.

Recommendation 5: Establish a practice that all corporate IT systems in current operation or under development, processing environments and support infrastructures (in-house or outsourced), and new contemplated technologies be assessed and continuously monitored for potential adverse impacts on the business. Reports are to be presented periodically to the executive IT management committee. Such action will signal that preventive thinking and responsible risk-reduction actions are as valued as risk-taking behavior and will encourage a more balanced view of IT throughout the organization. Such actions also should be viewed favorably by the board, stockholders, insurance carriers, and business partners. Those in the stock-growth-at-any-price crowd may not appreciate this type of conservative management and probably will not understand a risk management approach to IT. Those who are learning from the Y2K experience will see the necessity and support the effort.

MAKE IMPROVEMENTS TO IT MANAGEMENT

Pre–Year 2000 Thinking

The IT industry, as a whole, has a poor track record when it comes to delivering successful implementations of the technology. While some failures can be attributed to technical factors and to supplier or vendor problems, most must be laid at the feet of ineffectual corporate and project management of information assets and the enabling IT. The most available and penetrating audits of IT management and unsuccessful attempts to utilize informational assets at the enterprise level have been conducted over the years by the U.S. General Accounting Office (GAO), usually at the request of members of Congress. Note that a good number of audits report on private sector companies running government systems under contract. From an overall management perspective, the GAO consistently has identified the following problems as fundamentally contributing to IT project and management failures:

- Lack of top management commitment
- Inadequate planning and execution
- Abandonment of the project plan
- Inexperienced project managers
- Flawed technical approach
- Failure to anticipate advances in technology
- Failure to satisfy user needs
- Inadequate documentation
- Acquisition problems

While each of these appear to be separate areas of difficulty, they all concentrate their impact and directly affect the IT manager who must somehow orchestrate these, and other myriad issues, to deliver a successful system.

IT managers generally have been ill-prepared for the duties and responsibilities of this job. In the world of IT managers, few have formal business management training and even fewer are educated in the disciplines of IT best-practice management. Since successful IT management is learned primarily through working on successful projects, and not in a classroom setting, there is a shortage of managers who know how to be effective. Bad practices simply are passed from one project to the next because so few managers ever have been associated with a success. Or, often a manager comes in during the middle phases of an already-troubled project when there is little they can do to change the outcome short of starting over. Often, IT managers have been promoted to such positions as a reward to retain them with the company, or to demonstrate promotion policies. Many people become IT managers without proper preparation at subordinate management positions. Then there is the problem of recruiting IT managers from outside the company. This is a course of action fraught with danger for in this age of "resume inflation," it is very easy for prospective employees to misrepresent themselves, knowing how difficult it is for past employers to give candid appraisals for fear of legal action.

Finally, IT managers traditionally have been put into situations of great responsibility but very little authority. Regardless of the experience level of an IT manager, there is little chance for other than marginal success without the fully visible commitment and support of corporate executives. Lack of top management commitment is the number-one problem listed by the GAO and generally the number-one problem identified in the autopsy report of any failed IT initiative.

Top executive commitment can be demonstrated, if it is to be believed by IT managers who often must enforce unpopular or seemingly unnecessary system/software development or quality assurance and testing actions, only by requiring consistent adherence to the discipline of IT best practices and by supporting IT management in the enforcement of such discipline. Executive action to implement the recommendations suggested in this book would demonstrate such support and make possible the institutionalization of the lessons learned from the Y2K experience.

Additionally, implementation of the recommendations in this book will solve, to a great extent, the other problems identified by the GAO.

Post–Year 2000 Thinking and Practice

The most critical improvements that can be made in support of the management of IT are those that require and enforce forms of accountability. If anything is to be learned from the Y2K experience, it is that IT, like any other aspect of the business, must be pursued within a framework of accountability. It is increasingly clear that, throughout the many months leading up to the century turnover, the principle objective of IT vendors, service providers, and IT-intensive businesses was to disclaim responsibility for any adverse impacts resulting from date-processing problems. Intriguingly, non-IT business in general, when given the opportunity to counter the IT industry's intense lobbying for increased protection from accountability for Y2K–related problems, chose to stand by and let "safe haven" legislation become law.

Post–Y2K uses of IT and post–Y2K selection of IT providers will center on the issue of accountability, and companies that grasp the importance of this issue will become leaders in their industry. The remainder of this discussion concentrates on actions to be taken by the executive IT management committee that will bring accountability to IT and its uses within the corporation and with business partners.

REQUIRE DEVELOPMENT AND DELIVERY METHODOLOGIES

Pre–Year 2000 Thinking

Having just made it easier for IT vendors, suppliers, and service providers to evade responsibility for their products and actions through passage of Y2K safe haven laws, it will be interesting to see just how businesses intend to deal with their IT suppliers in the future and how IT service providers will be selected. It can be hoped that consumers of IT products and services will become more discerning and begin to satisfy their IT needs based on elements of product quality and on the reputation of companies known for excellence in all aspects of IT product and service management.

Before the Y2K experience most buyers gave little thought to how IT products were built. The quality movement of the late 1980s never really changed the buying habits of IT consumers, and it barely influenced the actual way software and system products were constructed. Both buyer and consumer stayed focused on new features and lower prices accompanied by appealing marketing promises that never fully materialized. Then there were the millions of consumers who had to go where the vendor led them. Once a vendor has a captive consumer, quality does not have to take a very high priority. Without competition, vendors can become very nonchalant about customer desires for quality software. Depending on the terminology used to describe quality, vendors can be selective as to where they concentrate their attention and efforts. If, for example, consumers are more influenced by the creative use of screen icons and know or care little about the importance of having current and accurate software documentation, guess where the vendor will concentrate the effort? Exhibit 2.4 defines a practical list of quality attributes. Each attribute is important to the overall characteristic of a software product or system, whether off-the-shelf or custom programmed. A quality software product or system cannot focus on just one or two quality attributes at the expense of others, because all of the attributes together describe a system that functions properly, is customer/user friendly, and can be modified and maintained easily and quickly by the keeper of the code. Ask about the problems experienced during the corporation's most recent systems upgrade. Inquire about the condition of systems and code that needed Y2K remediation action. The answers, if honestly given, probably will indicate that considerable and unnecessary difficulties were directly attributable to software that poorly satisfied one or more quality attributes—usually the problem is with lack of modular design to facilitate ease of maintenance and documentation for ease of modification, installation, and customer use.

Quality IT software systems and services are the product of a formal disciplined *system development process* (SDP). As introduced earlier, there are several popular renditions of this process, and all have existed for at least two decades. The SDP concept represents the best single available solution to the problem of developing and delivering quality and cost-effective systems and software. Executive management needs to inquire about the SDP being used by the corporation's software and system developers. Unless a standard process for the definition, creation, and delivery of systems is followed, the lack of knowledge about "how systems work" will continue to plague the next generation of IT application. The chaos many organizations endured with the Y2K experience will be repeated again and again whenever software or systems have to be retrofitted to accommodate new requirements. For example, some of the large retrofit projects upcoming in the next few years include completing the conversion to the Euro and the inevitable expansion of Social Security numbers and phone numbers. Each of these massive projects plus companies' routine software change requirements are best accomplished on systems and software that are the products of the disciplined adherence to a standard SDP. Even better would be to design corporate systems today to accommodate the future expansion, then retrofits will be unnecessary. Using the example of building a custom home, the SDP would be akin to the disciplined process and procedure that an architect employs for defining client requirement, when designing a structure that satisfies those requirements, and when using design documents to guide the work of construction contractors. The architect follows a path of requirements, specifications, ordering materials, contracting for assembly, and going through final inspection with those who have an interest in the final product.

During the course of events, the architect develops blueprints to guide the effort of construction personnel who assemble the components of the house that have satisfied the specifications. Specifications are expressions of expected quality and can be traced back to the desires of the homeowner or to some "code" used to set standards for construction and safety.

It is the same with successful IT systems, even to the extent of making major or minor modifications after the software system has been completed—but only with successful IT systems. Where the process and procedures of an SDP have not been followed, the orderly progression from requirements to a fully documented, quality-inspected final software system is haphazard at best and seriously deficient at worst. When modifications must be made to a deficiently constructed system, chaos prevails, and generally an additional and costly effort is required to determine just how a modification can proceed. It is like deciding to make a change, such as adding a picture window, to a nearly completed house but not knowing that the target wall happens to be load bearing. Why is this important piece of information lacking? Because the discipline of following and updating the architect's drawings was not followed or enforced—it was not documented in the blueprints.

Post–Year 2000 Thinking and Practice

Companies, in the post–year 2000 world, will strive to be able to defend against charges of system and software development negligence once the concept of the SDP and the discipline of software engineering are clear to the minds of juries. Once it is recognized that software and systems development is not magic, but rather the result of an orderly process of defining, designing, developing, and testing, all businesses will be forced to embrace and enforce an appropriately chosen SDP out of self-defense.

To be sure, some IT personnel will argue that the imposition of a process will stifle their creativity. Or they will argue, and be supported by the marketing department, that the comprehensiveness of an SDP is overkill and will delay time-to-market expectations. But what corporation needs creativity except during the design of the system? Creativity during development (i.e., programming and integration of software packages) is like allowing each construction worker to individually interpret the blueprint and make changes to "improve" the house.

Remember, the name of the IT game changes once accountability enters the scene. In anticipation of this shift, corporate executives need to take action to ensure that all future IT projects and system development initiatives are constructed according to some industry-recognized systems development process.

Recommendation 6: Establish policy that all corporate system and software developments and integration efforts be guided by a systems development process or methodology that incorporates the life-cycle phases of preparation, definition, design, development, deployment, and maintenance or the equivalent. Enforce its use.

Appendix B covers the essential technical and management action plans that need to be activated or otherwise accounted for during any systems or software development project or for any technology integration effort.

The model presented as Exhibit 5.1 portrays the framework whereby executives can visualize and grasp the many phases and technical and management activities that constitute a best-practices approach to a development or integration project. While the appendix provides greater detail, a brief explanation is appropriate here.

The framework is laid out in columns and rows. The rows indicate the phases of a development and/or integration effort, and the columns are comprised of management requirements and infrastructure risk monitoring elements. To increase the likelihood of success of an IT software/systems development project or a technology integration project, development personnel need to proceed down the rows in accordance with the various monitoring and action plans of the columns. The columns represent a specialized view or set of requirements for the system under development. Extend the lines separating the phases across the framework and we have a matrix. Within each box or cell formed by the intersection of the lines visualize a specific set of action items describing what is to occur regarding

Exhibit 5.1 Systems Development Process Framework

Life-Cycle Phases	MANAGEMENT REQUIREMENTS										
	Project Management Plan	Software Engineering Plan	Internal Controls Plan	Security Plan	QA & Testing Plan	CM Plan	Documentation Plan	Technology Transfer Plan	Training Plan	Infrastructure Risk Monitoring		
										Hardware	Software	Network
Preparation												
Definition												
Design												
Development												
Deployment												
Maintenance												

each management requirement at any particular phase of the project. For example: the column labeled "Security Plan" refers to the action of requiring that each of the project's analytic and development phases be influenced by the task of securing the system before it is put into operational status. This means that from an oversight perspective, executives should expect that specific action items of the security plan for the system under development correspond to the phases in the life cycle. The security plan would state what is to be accomplished during each phase of the life cycle for the software or system. This would mean that there are security action items to be accomplished during the preparation phase, the definition phase, the design phase, and so on, until the secured system is turned over to operational maintenance status. The security plan of the SDP framework ensures that security requirements affecting design and implementation actions are not lost in the totality of the effort or overlooked because of unsubstantiated assurances that "something is being done about security."

Use of the framework also forces attention to other elements of systems and software development management that usually get lost in general discussions of a project's life-cycle phase progression. Of these other management requirements, the most critical is the *quality assurance (QA) and testing plan.* To be effective, quality assurance and testing need to progress phase for phase with the execution of the *software engineering plan* for the technical system being constructed as the IT solution to the business requirement. This means that QA and testing activities need to be performed on the work products of the software engineering effort at each phase. If they are not performed, the risk of errors and defects going undetected as software development progresses rises, and the cost to fix problems later in the life cycle increases dramatically.

Equally important and directly related to executive-level IT risk monitoring (Appendix C) is the need for project-level monitoring of infrastructure risks that could adversely affect timely implementation of the system. Each project under development or resulting from the integration of multiple off-the-shelf products must monitor continually those physical components of the infrastructure upon which the completed project's work product will operate. Typically, this would mean anticipating support product upgrades, independently evaluating tested product reports, and monitoring support contractor viability for those hardware, software, and network elements upon which the business depends. At each major phase of the life cycle, a status check of each of these areas needs to be conducted to affirm that basic project risk assumptions are not changing.

The remaining management requirements (i.e., columns) of Exhibit 5.1 can be briefly defined as follows:

• *Project Management Plan.* This game plan for project and subproject managers ensures that the total effort will satisfy the business requirement by delivering a quality product within budget and time estimates. Budgets and time to finish are a product of analyses performed during the first two phases of the life cycle and then modified accordingly as the project progresses. At the execution level, all traditional process management tools would be employed to plan and monitor progress and to allocate resources as required. In a practical sense, a project manager who insists on having management requirement subplans from each management requirement area would have an effective method of project feedback and therefore would be less subject to surprises later in the project's schedule.

• *Software/System Engineering Plan.* This plan lays out the work tasks to build the technical solution to the business requirement in a disciplined and structured fashion using one of many methodologies such that each phase of the project builds on the work products of the previous phase. In other words, working backward from the final system under maintenance, the ease and speed with which maintenance changes can be performed is predicated on the deployment (installation) of a software/system that not only executes its code on the computer but was delivered having satisfied all elements of each management requirements plan. A system having been delivered in this condition meets all aspects of what the industry would generally judge to be a project developed according to "best practices."

Likewise, the successful deployment of the system depends not only on successful completion of code development but on the successful completion of each management requirements plan through the end of the development phase. If, for example, the project is late according to the documentation plan, then the system is not ready for deployment unless executives are willing to accept the risk of confused employees projecting a less than professional image to the customer, or confused system operators ill-prepared to run the system, or confused help-desk personnel ill-prepared to talk users through routine deployment questions.

To ensure the readiness of a software or systems product to progress to the next life-cycle phase, all planned activities of each management requirements plan need to be complete and any changes in the hardware, software, or network infrastructure need to be considered. This process can be monitored easily and time-efficiently by the IT executive committee once the management requirements plans have been formulated.

There will be conflicts. Marketing and sales, business development, and many other corporate centers of power will balk at this approach to managing IT the first time they must adjust their expectations rather than deliver a system before it is ready. This is why top management support for IT management improvement is so important. Improvement will not happen without such support because no CIO can withstand the pressures to cut corners and make accommodations, as have always been done in the past. It is likely that even executives cannot create, with a single edict, such fundamental change; that is why continuous involvement and oversight will be necessary until cultures change and the positive fruits from this approach begin to become evident. Remember, the opposite has already been proven. Lack of management direction creates influence in the opposite direction. In other words, management can prevent the use of best practices merely by not dictating their use. If the corporation truly desires to get IT projects under control, then the remaining management requirements plans are necessary.

• *Internal Controls Plan.* This plan sets forth the requirements for auditability and the need for internal controls operating within the system under development to ensure accounting rule consistency and data integrity. These are development actions that call for close coordination with the corporation's audit group and the external auditor. Internal controls represent an area beyond the expertise of most IT professionals, so qualified computer audit personnel need to be intimately involved whenever it is necessary to develop an internal controls plan. As with any business requirement that is being reduced to computer code, the internal control requirements need to progress in sync with the overall development of the software engineering plan or else they will be implemented improperly, if at all, and be ineffectual.

• *Security Plan.* Because of the critical importance of this issue, the framework includes it as a separate plan to encourage high-visibility monitoring. The security plan takes form after a security risk analysis is performed of the application being built and of the environment in which it will operate. While most infrastructure security measures provide a degree of access control, virus scanning, and disaster/recovery services, truly effective security is founded in the unique requirements of the business application. Thus, the security controls to be placed on a company-sensitive research and development application will be different from controls over the account receivables and different still from those controls placed on the parking lot permit system. This management requirements plan allows the unique security needs of the application under development to be defined, designed, developed, tested, and deployed as an integral yet separately tracked set of application specifications.

• *Quality Assurance and Testing Plan.* This plan ensures that quality characteristics that can be quantified or otherwise meaningfully expressed are present in the project's final work products, whether code, database, or documentation. This plan also identifies the action plan for the use of standard QA techniques and tools to ensure that best practices were properly employed during development and during all testing. Using a best-practices approach, initial QA activities and tests are accomplished by the developers themselves as they work through design and development issues. Later, independent QA reviews and final prerelease testing should be performed by a totally different group from the developers. The greater the risk posed by the release of flawed software or systems, the greater the necessary rigor required of the plan. QA and testing are areas where automated tools can be of great help. Tools, however, require a sizable investment in dollars and time and should be selected carefully to augment standardized QA and testing procedures required of the development group and any contractors supporting the project. Substantial quality improvements and project cost reductions can be demonstrated, by way of metrics, when QA and testing tools are used patiently and incorporated into all development efforts.

• *Configuration Management (CM) Plan.* This plan prescribes how each of the individual work products from the many activities of a development or integration project are to be controlled. This process of managing configurations means that at any moment in time and at any point of the life cycle, all system components and items under construction or being integrated can be identified and located in their most recent version. In a small- to medium-size development or integration undertaking, system components and items requiring configuration management easily number in the hundreds. On large projects a CM database may have thousands of entries. Without configuration management, projects spin out of control and the ability to judge actual progress becomes next to impossible because development actions do not necessarily proceed in unison. Components and items under development that, in the end product, must work together may take many paths to final assembly. One module of a program may skate through testing while a sister module runs into test difficulties and is forced to revisit previous steps of the development process in order to solve the problem. Configuration management is needed to maintain consistency or agreement among the system/software requirements, design, code, and test cases. When all of these elements are consistent, the developer has a "baseline" (i.e., the last known instance when all elements agreed with each other) of the system under development at a particular point in time. As a project nears completion, all baselines merge into one final tested and documented system baseline for user acceptance and deployment. Automated tools can be of benefit to configuration management. As with QA and testing tools, the payback dividends are well documented. As with other system management techniques, configuration management must be pursued with patience and exceptions cannot be allowed.

One of the major enforcement elements of CM is change control, a procedure whereby routine and emergency modifications to software are brought under a controlling process. Change control requires that all changes to the baseline of a system be analyzed for risk and for any adverse impact on other aspects of the operational business system. This type of procedure, if applied, prevents unknown, and therefore uncontrolled, changes to a system's baseline. Change control is absolutely essential to maintaining the integrity of software and databases and the stability and reliability of the hardware and network infrastructure.

• *Documentation Plan.* This plan specifies the documents that are to be generated during the course of the project. As stated earlier, documentation is the glue that holds the project together during times of staff turnover and ensures that replacement personnel do not make unnecessary interpretations. The more interpretations can be kept to a minimum, the easier it will be to stay consistent with the original design and with work products already completed. Without adequate and accurate documentation, progress between phases may be delayed as documents describing previous work products have to be researched for meaning and accuracy. It would be like handing incomplete blueprints and work order instructions to a subcontractor and expecting the work to be completed on time and according to original design intent. Of course, the worse case would be if the blueprints or the inaccurate and inadequate systems documentation were actually followed as if it were accurate. In such cases, the effects of the miscommunication between phases and workers may not be discovered until very late in construction, when only major and expensive retrofitting can meet the original intent—all because the discipline of documenting and reviewing work products was not enforced.

• *Technology Transfer Plan.* This plan defines the actions to be taken to ensure that employees/customers are ready to operate the system upon turnover. This plan must take into account the knowledge and skills gap between what the workforce currently is capable of and what effective and efficient operation of the new system demands. Too often, software and systems are programmed and delivered on the assumption that the customer has the same basic technical experience as the developer. If a certain level of increased technical sophistication is required of the customer, then the technology transfer plan should identify the means by which the less-sophisticated customer/user can become proficient. This is more than just training, and it applies more often to custom-developed solutions than to off-the-shelf packages. Technology transfer also applies to preparing the operational workplace to receive the new system. The hardware, operating system, software, and network support elements of the infrastructure need to be in place and operating successfully before newly developed software can be installed and turned over for production work. This requirement posed a huge challenge to solving the Y2K problem. While business systems needed to be remediated, the hardware operating systems and networks upon which they resided also needed Y2K upgrades. All of these changes were going on concurrently and had to be merged into a total operational system sometime just before 1 January 2000.

Similar problems present themselves with even routine development projects, especially if there is a planned deployment of a new system to many decentralized locations and hardware and software platforms are being upgraded at the same time. Technology transfers also may be quite complex if a number of different vendors are involved and extensive coordination is required. To be sure, not every IT project requires a technology transfer plan, but such plans are indispensable for any medium to large undertaking.

• *Training Plan.* This plan should be required to ensure that end users are properly educated and equipped to use the system successfully and efficiently in performance of their job duties. This plan must reflect not only technical aspects of the system but any workplace procedural changes as well. Attention should be focused once again on Exhibit 1.4, which illustrates all aspects of job training that may need modification when a new piece of software or a system is deployed into the organization.

• *Instrastructure and Risk Monitoring.* This is a critical element of the SDP framework since unknown changes to any of the elements upon which deployment depends could have adverse effects on timely fielding of the system. The infrastructure elements being monitored (i.e., hardware, operating systems software, and networks) also were included as items monitored in the IT risk management review model. These three technology elements plus inherent project risks represent areas of constant and very rapid change. Assumptions concerning the operational environment need to be revisited frequently and reassessed for validity or else new system deployments may experience delays and operational problems.

Three distinct uses for the SDP management approach should hold special interest for the executive members of the corporate IT management committee. First, the SDP framework or its equivalent will provide the controlling mechanism for guaranteeing the quality of all IT products and services developed by the corporation, whether for internal use or for delivery to a customer. Second, in preparing for the increased likelihood of future litigation following the Y2K experience, executives need to recognize that enforced use of the SDP, in some form or other, provides a best-practices proof of reasonableness when questions about due diligence in software systems management are raised; and when documenting evidence is requested to support actions taken and decisions made during the course of systems development or integration. (See Appendix D.)

Third, the SDP can be used as a tool to judge the maturity of the corporation's software and systems development capability or that of a business partner or IT provider of products and services.

A formal process for performing this type of evaluation has been developed by Carnegie-Mellon University's Software Engineering Institute (SEI) for the Department of Defense (DOD). The original purpose for the development of an evaluation model was the desire of the DOD to improve its own software development capability and that of its contractors. The capability maturity model (CMM), as it is known, evaluates the current software practices of an organization, ranks its capability on a progressive scale of 1 to 5, and then, based on the evaluation, provides feedback on necessary improvements to raise the overall CMM. Each of the levels is best described by the presence or lack of IT best practices governing the software, systems, or integration environment of the organization.

- *Level 1* is noted for a lack of any standard best-practice processes used during development. With level 1 organizations, IT development personnel do their own thing based on their previous experience. According to SEI statistics, 80 percent of software development organizations are at level 1. In other words, they are essentially unmanaged and are not using any of the software engineering and project management techniques and tools that have proven to deliver quality and cost-efficient systems.

- *Level 2* organizations have made attempts to adapt many of the techniques found in the SDP framework, but they are generally poor at enforcement and cannot replicate or repeat the use of the techniques from one project to another. Employees in level 2 organizations are still essentially on their own but are a little more sophisticated in their use of best practices. It is very much a project-by-project application of IT management practices as governed by the project manager. Executives have not, as yet, required the institutionalization of the management requirements of the SDP framework, although they may have begun to gather metrics data.

- *Level 3* organizations, which may account for fewer than 5 percent of all software and system developers, have adopted all aspects of the SDP framework and are now concentrating on improving their software engineering abilities as well as project management practices. There is considerable focus on training to improve individual skills and intergroup activities to facilitate coordination and knowledge exchanges.

- *Level 4* organizations have built a quality management and continuous improvement program mentality into the way they go about the business of software and systems development.

• *Level 5*, the "Holy Grail" of IT improvement, is centered not only on efforts to improve processes but on applying techniques and tools to prevent defects from occurring. The ultimate benefit from metrics efforts are now realized because organizations can be very effective in their resource estimating and project planning and also can use prior project data to better manage current workloads.

Recommendation 7: The Executive IT Management Committee should commission an evaluation of current corporate software development and maintenance capabilities using the SEI's capability maturity model.

Recommendation 8: In order to progress beyond level 1, establish a software development and systems management metrics program and begin building the databases of experiental data upon which higher levels of the CMM can be built.

It has been the premise of this discussion that the SDP is the most powerful single tool available to corporate executives for getting a handle on information technology in its many forms. Use of the SDP brings to IT an analytic integrity and developmental discipline that too often has been missing during the last three decades. For a developer of systems and software, the framework provides the discipline and control necessary to achieve the level of improvements in quality and reliability that post–year 2000 customers are going to demand. Yes, demand. The end result of Y2K safe haven statutes and stealthy changes to the Uniform Commercial Code may well be other than that intended. Such self-serving laws and actions, passed to further protect software and systems companies, may backfire and galvanize buyers of IT products and services to be more aggressive in their efforts to deal with the buyer beware reality of doing business with the IT industry. Buyers, for example, could begin to do a number of things to try to bring the playing field back into balance. First, they can make it known in their request for proposals that they will consider only those companies with a level 3 or 4 CMM rating. Second, buyers can require reviews of all system development plans and conduct documentation inspections as a project progresses. Buyers can require truly independent third-party validation, verification, and testing of system and software work products. This can be done for custom-developed software as part of the contract or as a separate contract. For packaged software, independent validation and verification of a vendor's release can be done through independent test labs or by common-user group collaboration. Buyers also can hold out for meaningful penalties in case of contract delay or cancellation—penalties that reflect actual businesses losses, not just token fines.

In other words, buyers must protect their corporate self-interests by becoming much more circumspect and critical in their dealings with IT vendors and providers. If a corporation's only protection is going to be the contract, then the contract needs to require, and to confirm, that specific best practices be employed during specified life-cycle phases—preferably those that are standard for the corporation. If the IT vendor or provider balks at this or seeks to charge extra (i.e., for doing it right), then shop around.

This process of making demands will change the way IT vendors and providers do business, if they want the business.

Some IT vendors and providers are so huge and powerful that the average corporate customer feels helpless to change the nature of the relationship or get quality products and services. But this condition already existed at least once during the short history of IT—back in the 1960s. Eventually, the mighty vendor was humbled by user groups that unified and made their demands known, competitors who capitalized on the situation, and a new invention called the personal computer.

CUSTOMER RELATIONS AND TECHNICAL SUPPORT

Pre–Year 2000 Thinking

During the pre–year 2000 period, customer relations and technical support constituted two very troubled aspects of the IT industry. Both have come to prominence because of the shortfall in the quality of products sold and poor services provided. In most IT companies, customer relations has become synonymous with crisis management and the damage control required after a defective product has been shipped or after a services contract fails to make a deliverables schedule or delivers analytic products of such poor quality as to be unusable by the customer. Suddenly, the customer comes into focus and the organization vaguely remembers the total quality management (TQM) briefings and facilitated sessions of the 1980s where the customer was declared king and everyone signed a corporate purpose statement. Then it was back to business as usual. We know this to be true because of the Software Engineering Institute estimates that over 80 percent of developers are still at the initial level of CMM. While some industries, notably automobile manufacturing, made quantum improvements in quality, the movement barely caused a ripple in the IT industry. That is because the IT industry was too busy innovating and getting new customers to accept poor-quality software and systems. Apparently reluctant to embrace the marketing fact of life that it costs far more to get a new customer than to retain an existing one, IT vendors have too often pursued strategies that appear designed to create disgruntled customers. Belatedly, vendors then attempt to deal with what were preventable problems by creating trouble desks or help desks, usually staffed by junior employees to accomplish the nearly impossible task of solving an immediate problem while salvaging what could already be a bad customer relations situation for the company. To appreciate the absurdity of this condition, one needs to see the situation clearly. Essentially, senior, highly compensated managers and technical specialists mismanage the development or integration of a product or service to such an extent that significant corporate resources have to be employed in attempting to solve problems after the customer has purchased what was portrayed to be a finished product. And what corporate resource is being assigned to what is really an unnecessary task? Not those responsible for the situation, but much junior people who are placed in the delicate position of having to field product questions for which there may be no answers, while at the same time trying to navigate potentially rough waters to retain some semblance of customer sensitivity and service. Then, to add insult to injury, the customer, who was king during the quality management seminar, is often forced to pay the bill by using the (900) number the corporation supplied for customer purposes.

Post–Year 2000 Thinking and Practice

Tailored customer services and technical support, as a follow-on value-added activity to better utilize an already stable and quality product, are services that customers are willing to pay for. But the practice by some vendors of viewing these two postdeployment activities as an extension of the testing and quality assurance phase of development needs to be examined. While the IT group within a corporation may tolerate this, executives need to discourage the practice since it constitutes a hidden subsidy to the vendor and makes corporate assimilation of new products that much more difficult and threatening to the business.

Recommendation 9: Executive members of the IT management committee need to rededicate themselves, the IT group, support contractors, and suppliers to the practices of quality management and continuous process improvement. Promotion and reward systems need to be aligned with this emphasis. Executive management must act as final arbiter when there are conflicts among quality, expediency, and the customer.

IT VENDOR AND SUPPLIER SELECTION

Pre–Year 2000 Thinking

The last 20 to 30 years of technological evolution have created a world of extensive, though not readily apparent, dependencies. Nowhere is this truer than with information technology and the use of computers. Traditional management techniques have not kept pace with this evolution and will require augmentation over the next couple of decades to be more effective. One of the areas needing attention, which was brought to light because of the Y2K experience, deals with the selection of future IT suppliers, service providers, and outsourcers. Until rather recently, IT source selections were driven primarily by technical issues as evaluated by technical personnel on a purely technical basis. Insufficient attention was given to examining business issues and the management processes that competing vendors employed during construction of their product. There was a fundamental belief, on the part of the buyer, that the IT company, as the expert, knew what it was doing and that trust was necessary when entering into a contract. Besides, few people had any idea what to evaluate or how to conduct such an evaluation.

In the wake of Y2K, many organizations will begin to feel as if their trust in the vendor community has been misplaced. Assurances that products and systems were compliant have proven to be untrue or only partially true. Or the product was not compliant but it was "ready" or perhaps "compliant capable" or "compliant with exceptions." It has been reported that as high as 50 percent of software vendors made compliance claims that did not stand up to independent testing. In such an environment, trust is hard to maintain. Many vendors and service providers are being greatly harmed and will have a difficult time recovering their reputation for trust-worthiness—if they ever had one.

So if trust in vendors and service providers is at a low point, how can a business executive proceed to select the next generation of IT products and services? What must the executive management committee do to better protect corporate interests and not continue to be victimized by promises and unsubstantiated product claims?

Post–Year 2000 Thinking and Practice

There are several things that corporations can do in the absence of vendor trust. To recap:

- Expect and require vendor adherence to a system development process that satisfies all the requirements of the framework (Appendix B).
- Require a CMM level of at least 3.
- Negotiate meaningful penalties for nonperformance that reflect actual corporate losses.
- Support common-user groups and use these to bring pressure on vendors to improve quality of products and services. As an example, recently, IT managers have decided to use their collective buying power to improve the usability of vendor-supplied software before they recommend purchase for their corporate clients. They are devising a standard way to measure software usability by working with industry software publishers and the National Institute of Standards and Technology (NIST). This is a good example of the power of organized buyers.

Finally, require not just marketing demonstrations of vendor products but the execution of performance benchmarks that reflect the workloads and unique characteristics of the companies' business applications. This technique is more expensive and usually has been reserved for large IT applications that include hardware buys, but in an atmosphere of limited trust, this approach should be more liberally applied than previously. Vendors wishing to reestablish themselves will cooperate with this technique and be thankful for the opportunity.

Recommendation 10: Establish IT process management criteria for selecting future vendors and suppliers. Include the capability maturity model evaluation method, independent verification and testing of products, and performance benchmarking. Establish selection evaluation committees with membership that represents all stakeholders to every project.

OUTSOURCING IT SUPPORT

Pre–Year 2000 Thinking

Closely related to the issue of IT vendor and supplier selection is the increasingly popular practice of putting under contract major portions or even the entire IT/computer processing support activity. Two rationales usually are offered: (1) it is more cost-effective than continuing to do IT in-house, and/or (2) the company was "never very good with this IT stuff so let's hire some professionals to do it for us."

Both justifications have wide appeal because there is an element of truth in both. At the same time, both rationales are very simple statements of a far more complex situation that requires extremely careful analysis that must now include what has been learned from the Y2K experience.

First, IT/computer processing support is not inexpensive no matter how the work is accomplished. If a comprehensive economic analysis baseline of the IT work to be performed has been established, bidding contractors will find it harder to *appear* more cost-effective than in-house task accomplishment. The more comprehensive the cost model, the harder it becomes to bid substantially lower costs by being able to ignore expenses not asked for by the model. The vendor-preferred scenario is to have unknown and unevaluated items of expense that can surface after contract award when there is little risk of losing the contract.

A comprehensive cost model is constructed by paying careful attention to all foreseeable life-cycle expenses identified during the operational analysis of the feasibility study. For example, those costs associated with maintaining and administering the operational system in production are wildly understated in most economic analyses. Under an outsourcing arrangement these will constitute the majority of the costs; but since they are directly related to the quality and the production readiness of the system to be in operation, a proposing contractor cannot bid intelligently unless an evaluation of existing systems and in-house conditions is allowed. This is generally not practical since adequate documentation does not exist. Without such an analysis, outsource providers are forced to keep lowering their bids through a negotiation process that blindly pits contractors against each other. If contracting officials are not aware of the underlying technical difficulties associated with this approach, they will unwittingly force the bidding downward to the point where reputable contractors will bow out and the company will be left with what is jokingly referred to as the lowest bidder. Seeking a low bid is a worthy goal as long as there are few performance surprises later in the contract period and few preventable cost escalations because of the forced earlier bidding. Due to the nature of competitive acquisition policies, the inherent difficulty in constructing realistic cost models, the even greater difficulty in attempting to develop value-added models, and the scarcity of IT-savvy contracting officials, IT managers generally dread the award of *any* contract to the lowest bidder, let alone an outsourcing deal.

Successful IT outsourcing results from intelligent bid preparation, proposal evaluation, and contracting. The success of these items depends on a clear and accurate understanding, by all parties, of the exact nature of the work to be accomplished and a clear and accurate understanding of all aspects of the business and IT environment within which the outsourcer will have to operate.

What has been learned from the Y2K experience is that many organizations were not able to assemble clear and accurate baselines of their IT assets and operating environments without a significant inventory effort. Ideally, these newly assembled Y2K baselines, if now being kept current using configuration management and change control techniques, should make outsourcing less risky since all the information needed to bid, evaluate, and contract intelligently will be available. If, however, these baselines are not being kept up to date and accurate, outsourcing initiatives will remain high risk since intelligent bidding, evaluating, and contracting will not be possible and the lowest bidder phenomenon will continue to prevail.

The second rationale for outsourcing (i.e., we do not do IT very well, therefore . . .) needs to be approached carefully because this reasoning could result in several different situations, each with varying impacts on the company. First, depending on the nature of the IT work being considered for outsourcing, the idea can either provide a clear improvement or pose a threat to the life of the company. Before the Y2K experience, few organizations or senior executives thought about their IT applications using terms like "mission-critical" or "mission-sensitive." Unless the organization had experienced a recent computer-related business interruption, IT processing was just something that always seemed to get done. Unless the company's revenues were directly dependent on on-line transaction processing, the term "mission-critical" was not normally associated with IT. The term was reserved for such business activities as obtaining an increase in a line of credit or finalizing a merger.

Along came Y2K and corporations found that they were very closely tied to other companies and that other companies were highly dependent on them. And the source of the dependencies have turned out to be the IT systems that few executives gave a second thought before now. Today corporations find themselves in a maze of system dependencies while discovering that many of the IT systems are not being managed as other corporate systems are managed. Sounds exactly like the reason cited for outsourcing (i.e., we do not do IT very well, therefore . . .), except now the mission-critical nature of the systems are known and it is also known that no one is terribly confident how they really work. And by the way, all those other corporate activities that were thought to be well managed—also depend on IT.

It may well be that the corporation does not do a very good job of IT management; but does the company dare to create an even greater dependency by contracting out mission-critical processes when it does not understand how the systems really work? Remember, without the knowledge to conduct an intelligent outsourcing initiative, the company could end up in a lowest bidder situation and be worse off than before.

Post–Year 2000 Thinking

To be successful, outsourcing needs to originate from proper motivation and be influenced by the new sense of risk that Y2K IT dependencies have demonstrated. Proper motivation for entering into an outsource arrangement will focus on making long-term improvements and efficiencies to IT support activities through establishment of stable business relations with IT support providers. Such relationships will revolve around two issues: fair and equitable treatment of existing corporate IT employees, and the corporate ability and knowledge base to monitor the IT management and performance of the outsource provider.

Fair and equitable treatment of those corporate IT employees, subject to the consequences of an outsourcing, is not only morally right, it is necessary from a business survival perspective. In light of the poor management conditions now known to exist in many IT support organizations, to invite the wrath of disgruntled employees who possess, in their heads, the process knowledge of the business would be foolhardy.

The Y2K experience has demonstrated the great dependency businesses have on the goodwill of current IT employees. Employee loyalty is certainly subject to change during a time of upheaval brought by a move to outsource. The company is at its most vulnerable during such a time, and great efforts must be made to allay employees' fears and retain their support.

Outsourcing needs to be part of a much larger strategy for improving overall corporate capabilities to use business information and IT processing assets for the long-term benefit of the company, shareholders, and employees. When embarking on discussions concerning the plausibility and benefits of outsourcing, care must be taken not to take a simplistic economic view and rather to balance short-term cost-cutting monetary gains with the need to prevent unacceptable dependencies and vulnerabilities from developing.

The prevention of unacceptable dependencies in the working arrangement with an outsourcer addresses the issues of being able to monitor the outsourcers technical, process, and performance management. If a company contemplating outsourcing cannot do a competent job of monitoring outsourcer performance, the contract should not be let. If a company contemplating outsourcing cannot competently evaluate the technical and process management of the provider, the contract should not be let. As Y2K is showing, contracts and warranties seem to provide insufficient protection when a corporation's livelihood is at stake and cannot substitute for retaining enough core system employees to ensure continuity of business processes regardless of outsourcer performance.

In the wake of Y2K, outsourcing will be reexamined in the light of risky dependencies, and companies will rethink its appropriateness. When determined to be appropriate, executives must see to it that sufficient employee expertise and IT management capability still exists in the organization to ensure that the company can never be put at risk by the outsourcer contractor's inability to perform or properly manage IT.

Recommendation 11: Commission a review of all existing and pending company outsource arrangements to identify any risky dependencies or vulnerabilities that could threaten the viability of the corporation. For pending outsource arrangements, require that a comprehensive feasibility analysis be performed to allow for intelligent bidding, evaluation, and contracting.

Recommendation 12: Review all existing and pending outsource projects and plans to ensure adequacy of employee numbers and skills sufficient to monitor and manage the outsourcer.

IT PERSONNEL MANAGEMENT

Pre–Year 2000 Thinking and Practice

The IT labor market is tight and getting tighter. According to a 1999 Commerce Department report, the growth rate for computer scientists, systems analysts, and computer engineers will increase 100 percent for the decade ending 2006. That translates into 1.3 million new IT workers to fill new jobs and replace workers leaving the field or retiring. The Society for Information Management (SIM) says the current labor shortage is the most severe in 50 years, and executives expect it to continue well into the next century. It is estimated that 12 percent of all IT jobs are unfilled, and of these open positions 37 percent result from employee turnover. It appears that the labor shortage is having a negative impact on projects and ultimately on profits. It was reported in 1998 that 90 percent of projects were being delayed or were incomplete as a result of shortages.

Historically, there always has been a shortage of IT workers primarily because technical breakthroughs always stayed ahead of attempts by universities, government, and businesses to train in the myriad of evolving languages and processing techniques. This has resulted in an employment market where skilled, knowledgeable, and experienced people are easily placed and where companies, without effective human resource and IT management, can find themselves susceptible to the key-person syndrome.

Typically, many IT companies and IT-dependent corporations do not manage their IT personnel so as to reflect the dependency the organization has on them. Earlier I discussed the ways in which IT people sometimes are perceived by reviewing terminology used to describe them. And even though IT employees generally are well paid, often they are considered second-class citizens by other corporate employees and by managers. Faced with the reality, however, that IT personnel are easily employable, hold special knowledge upon which the corporation depends, and often are perceived in disparaging ways, special attention needs to be given to their management.

Conventional practice has been to recruit IT personnel as needed for a specific project requiring specialized skills. Once the project is complete, oftentimes the employee is let go. This scenario is the norm with both IT product and service companies and is becoming more commonplace among IT-intensive corporations. While viewed as desirable by some IT personnel, many others wish for more stability than the role of contract help offers them. The combined forces of technical specialization coupled with the movement to outsourcing have conspired to make difficult the creation and maintenance of a steadfast IT workforce. Yet, the IT-dependent and vulnerable corporation needs a steadfast group of IT professionals to support its goals and objectives, not hourly employees doing piecework and then leaving.

During the last two decades people in IT have tended toward three career paths. First are those who pursued the technical track of the industry, attempting to stay current with new manifestations of computing and being proficient within vendor product lines. Second were those that followed the technology management track, advancing through projects of increasing complexity and budget size. It has been within these first two tracks that the Peter principle has been observed most often. The principle states that people are advanced within an organization until they reach their level of incompetence. In the case of the IT technology track, promotion to management positions often has occurred in order to provide status rewards beyond those available in the technical track. Usually, promoting people into management positions without adequate preparation has the undesirable effect of denying the organization the skills of a highly competent technical person while saddling it with a new manager of questionable quality and experience.

The third career track, IT business development and corporate business management, was pursued by those desiring the rewards of product sales commissions and corporate officer remuneration and standing.

These three career paths are frequently at cross-purposes when customer satisfaction, product quality, or project accountability are at issue. For example, an IT manager and technical specialists working directly for an IT-intensive corporation often find themselves at odds with an IT vendor or service provider who is producing or delivering poor-quality software, systems, or support services. Likewise, IT managers responsible for product or service delivery can find themselves in conflict with their own business development and sales managers who are making unrealistic product and schedule promises.

These distinctions and the problems that can exist between members of the same industry are important because they revolve around IT business philosophy, practice, and quality and ethical issues that many IT professionals find highly problematic. For progress to be made in the post–year 2000 period, executive management must be aware of such distinctions and not stereotype IT workers inappropriately..

Post–Year 2000 Thinking

Management of IT personnel resources will prove critical in the period following 1 January 2000. All the attention to process management, risk identification and mitigation, quality assurance, and supplier/vendor management will amount to little without a strategic vision and plan on how to integrate IT professionals into the corporation such that all employees have a sense of shared purpose and belonging. However, it is that IT personnel management policies evolve over the next few years, they need to assume the following employee/employment realities:

• Shortages of IT qualified personnel will continue, which will increase pressure on traditional human resource recruitment hiring and retention practices.

• Continue to expect a considerable amount of job hopping from those choosing the technical career path as the importance of resume experience with new languages and products continues. Expect increasing difficulty in determining the truly experienced applicant from the resume inflator and develop recruitment screening and hiring standards to assist with this difficult task.

• Regardless of the final outcome of Y2K problems, expect an increase in disaffection among younger IT employees as the shortcomings of their elders' management styles begin to surface. This is the generation that just witnessed their parents being laid off as part of the merger mania of the 1980s and 1990s, and they begin the new millennium with little faith in the concept of corporate loyalty. Their sense of company loyalty is receiving yet another blow as they see the traditional retirement plans of older workers being threatened in the name of plan *portability.* At a time when loyalty is essential to the corporation, it may be in very short supply.

• Expect the IT organization to be the scapegoat for any remaining Y2K problems and to be both fairly and unfairly blamed for the business and economic difficulties that result. Executives should strive not to take the easy way out and blame IT employees for what has been primarily a management problem.

In formulating new IT personnel human resource management policies and practices, corporate executives should consider a number of things.

First, do not unconsciously blame today's IT worker for the oversights and omissions of yesterday's IT and corporate management that led to the Y2K and other problems. Do begin to manage IT like any other aspect of the business and demand accountability. Recognize that while the current generation of IT workers may feel a general distrust of the corporation for what occurred to their parents, they want to belong to something larger than themselves and sense purpose in their employment. Their generation is as idealistic as any other and wants to labor for goals worthy of their time and effort. Money may be a poor second to what the current generation of workers wish to accomplish. Challenge them with the importance of IT and their contribution to the business and society.

One extremely positive thing that corporate executives can do is to jealously guard the time of their IT employees. This can be accomplished by demanding adherence to the chosen SDP. This will force system development decisions to be made in the prescribed analytic sequence, thus facilitating the productive use of human resources. Doing this, of course, also will result in a better-quality system for the corporation. Poorly managed IT projects are very wasteful of employee time as prior work products are constantly being revisited to determine their appropriateness and validity.

In this condition projects do not follow the analytic sequence of an SDP, are not subjected to QA reviews, and are not correctly documented. Even if overtime is paid under certain conditions, employees generally experienced a great deal of *waiting* time. Occasionally, this is necessary, but if it occurs repeatedly due to poor project planning or because of time wasted in correcting preventable defects, employees, especially those with family obligations, will begin looking for more favorable work conditions.

With regard to conflicts surrounding SDP discipline and the equally important need for creative employee problem solving, both are important and can be integrated successfully if the creative energy is primarily directed toward the problem definition and solution design phases of the SDP. These are the exciting activities of a development effort and provide ample opportunity for individual and team collaborations. If management encourages creativity during these phases, it is easier to gain employee acceptance of the need for increased process discipline in the latter phases of programming, testing, system deployment, and maintenance. In fact, employees will see the need to protect the integrity of their systems solution from uncontrolled changes initiated by others who were not part of the original, and creative, effort. Employees may even come to accept the less glamorous aspects of development, such as QA, testing, and documentation, as ways of protecting their creation. While executive management must dare to control the progress of development and integration projects and demand accountability, such controls are by no means incompatible with employee desires for creative satisfaction. Both aspects of IT management need to be merged into the proper context of responsible computing.

To improve IT employee retention, it is important to adopt a cadre concept and purposefully design an IT workforce with distinct career paths built around the core competencies the company itself must retain to compete successfully. For each organization, there are certain knowledges, skills, and experiences that should not be subject to outsourcing. These positions are central to the business and represent those areas where employee turnover can threaten company viability. To the extent that these vital positions include IT activities, exclude them from outsourcing consideration. Create for these employees a clearly identified and mentored path to greater responsibilities and rewards. To the degree that IT employees feel a sense of belonging to the overall search for corporate success, they will respond loyally. If they sense they are merely skilled laborers, their loyalty will follow the dollar.

In designing a cadre, required job functions and not individual employees should be the focus. Design the progression of a "virtual" employee through the required and desired assignments needed to gain the requisite skills, knowledges, and experience that a position's competency demands. Make these career paths known at time of recruitment and use them to design individual employee development plans. These plans should be used to set goals and objectives for each performance period. Annual evaluations should be based, at least in part, on progress made by the employee against the plan.

Mentoring as well as work task supervision can be viewed as the vehicle for implementing a career path program. Work assignments and mentors should be changed periodically to achieve the desired experiences required of an employee's career path.

An integral part of the individual development plan for IT employees recognizes the need to subsidize continuing education. The current practice of many IT product developer and service companies is to pay for continuing technical training in exchange for a time commitment from the employee or repayment of tuition should the employee leave. This seems to work well enough for technology companies but may need to be modified to include nontechnical education for IT employees desiring better knowledge of the core business in an IT-dependent company. This would make the IT employee much more valuable from a business sense and would fit well into a career path program.

Another aspect of the cadre approach would be to mix IT work assignments with an occasional period of time doing some other corporate job that has direct customer contact. This idea, borrowed from the earlier advice given by Robert Townsend, would familiarize IT employees with the revenue-producing parts of the business, sensitize them to the work environment of those fellow employees out on the line, and allow them to see the fruits of their IT labors. Many IT employees never see the end results of their efforts and therefore do not have the sense of ownership and pride that contributes to high morale. While this concept may not lend itself to the IT products or service company, another idea that should be considered entails the creation within the company of a *technology and continuous improvement center.* A technology center is an efficiently run overhead activity where employees bring their recent project experiences to bear on the problem of continually improving the products and services of the company. There new technologies, techniques, and products can be examined for company use. It is where *capability maturity model* work can take place. The technology center also can serve as semi-independent verifier of project deliverables and work being done by other employees for clients. In this capacity the center can perform a vital quality assurance function.

A technology and continuous improvement center should be staffed from all IT and appropriate business unit employees on a rotating basis for a set period between work assignments. The size of the center, of course, must be appropriate to company size and revenues and should be justified not only for its contribution to product innovation, quality, and work process improvements but also for its positive effect on employees. Employees, rotating through the center, get unique opportunities to contribute to the company and a greater sense of worth and belonging. They also are introduced to aspects of computing technology and management that they may never experience on their workaday technical assignments.

Implementation of a technology and continuous improvement center requires an executive vision consistent with goals that are longer range than just next quarter's profit-and-loss statement. The rationale for such activities can be found in the works Edward Deming, Philip Crosby, and other quality management experts who have concentrated on work process improvements as the key to sustained productivity and increased profit ratios. It has long been recognized that defects can be reduced by focusing on the work processes of the organization. The overall savings from not having to correct defective products or perform rework go directly to the bottom line. A technology center, properly implemented, can provide such contributions to the bottom line and become a major factor in employee satisfaction and retention.

Compensation policy will come under great pressure in the period following Y2K. The shortages of skilled and experienced IT workers will continue to fuel an ever-rising spiral of wage increases, which in turn keeps turnover high in companies where other elements contributing to employee satisfaction are lacking. IT companies and IT-dependent corporations cannot win this game. Even IT employees lose if they change jobs too frequently. Only the headhunters win.

Against this backdrop, what course of action should executives foster regarding compensation and the IT employee? The simplest approach is to promote a policy of local geographic competitiveness coupled with rewards tied to performance. Easier said than done, however, with an industry beset by the problems that have so far been cataloged. Since there are few standard job descriptions and no widely accepted professional standards, defining acceptable performance and arriving at compensation decisions can too easily become personality based. Personality-based reward systems, while difficult to avoid, can destroy an IT organization. While management takes great solace in the confidentiality of its payroll file, there are few secrets in an IT organization and virtually none when it comes to salaries. Openness should be the rule with the salary range of an employment category available to all. Thus, it would be known to all that a senior systems analyst makes between $65,000 and $92,000 if working in Washington, DC, or that an entry-level programmer makes between $32,000 and $40,000 if working in Chicago. An annual rate increase policy tied to performance ratings should be published each year for all employees to see. The same for bonuses, again tied to performance.

Determining performance becomes the key to a fair and defensible compensation policy. This book has emphasized the benefits of metrics. Once again, metrics can contribute to managing the problem of fair compensation. To be sure, not every IT activity can be reduced to a set of measurements upon which compensation should be calculated. But it would seem reasonable at least to reward the data entry professional who consistently inputs greater numbers of transactions, without an increase in error rates, than the person who is less productive, and the programmer who can write a greater number of error-free compiled lines of code, given an equal complexity level, than the programmer who delivers fewer lines of code. While the latter example may prove contentious at times, it is preferable to rewarding each programmer the same regardless of defect rates. To the extent that measurement applies to the job under study, proficiency improvements can be documented and subjectivity in performance evaluations reduced. Measurements even can assist in career path and personal administration. If a performance reduction is noted, an employee can be scheduled for remedial training or for counseling.

Individual performance plans, based on applicable and reasonable metrics, should be developed for each employee for the reporting period. For IT employees, a visible link to their individual development plans is necessary so that performance for the company and career advancement are viewed together.

The coordination of individual development plans, individual performance plans, and compensation demonstrates to IT employees that they are valuable and are indeed an important member of the larger corporation. All of these rather difficult undertakings will be needed to build and retain a steadfast and loyal IT corporate workforce after the year 2000.

A question often asked of those seeking to increase the IT employee's sense of responsibility is whether the time has come to make IT a profession. This question has been debated for at least 25 years. There are, in fact, IT professional associations that promote professional behavior among their members and encourage adherence to a code of ethics. The Association of Computing Manufacturers, the Society for Information Management, the Quality Assurance Institute, and others have a code of ethics to which members subscribe and that form the core of the IT professionalism movement as it is now constituted. Membership in professional associations definitely seems to improve the performance of members, especially if the association is centered on a specific IT practice area such as QA, security, configuration management, and project management. Membership allows a sharing of lessons learned and a refining of the techniques used in job execution. Membership in professional societies also assists employers in the selection of employees for job vacancies. The fact that contractor employees hold professional memberships also gives additional assurances to contractor clients that IT personnel working their account are at least professionally active for the good of their own careers.

What membership in professional associations or the creation of an IT profession cannot do is to greatly improve the overall track record of IT project success and product quality, unless the IT professional is self-employed and can exert considerable control over the conditions of task performance. In employee status, however, the IT professional has considerably less influence and generally is constrained by the business behavior and practices of his or her employer. If the employing company does not adhere to best practices and enforce their use on projects, there is little the IT professional can do except to quit and seek employment elsewhere. If, for example, the employing company cuts corners on systems testing and documentation, there is little the individual professional can do except to document the situation and look for another job. Recording the specifics of unprofessional corporate actions may, in fact, be the only defense an IT professional will have should legal action be brought against the employing company for product or IT service deficiencies. This is because any employing company behaving in such manner undoubtedly will seek to place blame on "professional" IT employees who were working the account. Having made it impossible to deliver a system or service according to best practices, the employing IT company will scapegoat its IT professional employees by claiming the problems were their fault—that they were professionals and therefore knew better and were responsible for the defective product or service.

Recognition of IT as a profession would create a two-edged sword. On one hand, greater prestige would accrue to the IT worker; but with that prestige would come added responsibilities that few would be able to live with easily because of their employee status. The better approach will be to hold IT product and service companies to professional standards and not pretend to overcome IT deficiencies by simply holding the individual IT worker responsible for things he or she cannot influence short of whistle blowing.

Finally, after Y2K, IT employees who have been involved in the many months of remediation, testing, and reintegration of production systems are going to be close to exhaustion. If a period of corporate IT retrenchment following Y2K is necessary, these same people will be expected to become involved because of their now-intimate knowledge of the systemic relationship among business units and any still-existing date code problems. The challenge of revitalizing this group of employees for yet another critical task needs some consideration. To further complicate matters, Y2K support contractors are probably long gone by this time, and the entire workload will fall on the corporate IT staff.

This period of retrenchment, to be described in the next section, will make great demands on existing staff at a time when business unit managers will be expecting that backlogged IT initiatives be launched.

The executive challenge is twofold. First, depending on the severity of Y2K impact on the company, executives must prioritize IT retrenchment tasks with backlogged IT initiatives to achieve a mix that will allow the company to move forward competitively while at the same time solve IT technology and management problems that, if left unsolved, will adversely impact all future IT operations. Second, executives will need to give special attention to retention and reward system issues for those employees saddled first with Y2K tasks and now with assignments to clean up the IT shop and implement internal control processes before they can move on to new technology projects. As related previously, experience with contemporary technologies and new technology solutions is critical to most IT employees for career advancement. To withhold new technology projects from Y2K veterans will almost certainly be seen as having an adverse effect on the individual. And yet the retrenchment activity is critical and must be accomplished for the good of all concerned. The executive key to success for retrenchment assignments is to make sure that all employees are in fact involved—no one is exempt from retrenchment assignments. Each business unit manager and IT manager must be made responsible for a retrenchment activity and for getting the deficient area up to specification. All IT employees will perform work assignments to get the deficient areas up to best-practice levels of performance. Again, the Carnegie-Mellon Software Engineering Institute's capability maturity model and Appendix B can be used to guide these efforts; and it must be clearly understood that all employees are expected to participate as assignments are made. Even corporate executives will be involved as they establish their executive IT management committee and begin their executive risk management review process.

In the final analysis, the IT personnel problem posed by retrenchment and the company's return to basics may not materialize unless the effort comes to be seen as a corporate team undertaking. The sooner the retrenchment tasks are completed, the sooner everyone can pursue new technology projects.

Recommendation 13: Commission an analysis of current human resource policies to determine their effectiveness regarding IT employees. Concentrate the review on those human resources practices needed to recruit, hire, train, compensate, utilize, and promote a workforce that will grow in company loyalty.

Recommendation 14: Consider the creation of a cadre of IT employees to protect the company from the risks of outsourcing and contractor dependence. Design the cadre around those IT functions that must be preserved to guarantee continued corporate operations regardless of outsourcing contractor performance.

Recommendation 15: Consider the creation of a technology and continuous improvement center chartered with innovating and improving the company's

system products, services, and work processes. Treat the center as an overhead activity staffed, on a rotating basis, by IT employees and appropriate business unit employees.

ESTABLISHING IT MANAGEMENT BASICS—A PERIOD OF RETRENCHMENT

Pre–Year 2000 Thinking and Practice

Prior to the Y2K experience, little in the history of the IT industry had ever forced the adherence to good information technology management practice. Except for the individual professionalism of a given company or because of the high risks associated with a particular application, such as space shuttle programs, most IT software and systems have been developed and delivered with less than adequate attention given to quality and long-term maintainability. "First to market" has been the battle cry and "keep the overhead down" the motto. This reality, as previously noted, led to most of the problems associated with the Y2K experience and will continue to plague both IT and IT-dependent corporations far into the twenty-first century unless changed.

Post–Year 2000 Practice

Addressing this reality will result in the need for business and government users of IT to establish or resurrect the fundamental IT management and technology activities referred to throughout this book as best practices. This retrenchment effort will be needed to prevent the runaway complexity of future IT developments from creating an endless series of situations similar to the Y2K experience. A recommended retrenchment effort, for most organizations, will demand that the following best-practice implementation actions be undertaken and institutionalized:

- A systems development process (SDP) must be adopted and enforced by the corporation for use by internal systems developers as well as contractor personnel. The process should emphasize the feasibility study.
- The SDP must require the comprehensive management of all phases of systems development, quality assurance, security, software engi-

neering, documentation, and any other aspect of best practices common to the corporation's competitors.

- Inventories of computing assets must be kept current, requiring the creation of configuration management controls.
- All changes to any software or hardware system or operational configurations must be controlled to ensure that adequate quality assurance has been exercised, including comprehensive testing.
- Systems and software documentation needs to be brought up to date before proceeding with new modifications to Y2K compliant systems.
- All applications software should be matched against business systems needs and unneeded systems should be purged.
- All IT supplier and business partners need to be assessed for overall adherence to IT industry best practices and any standards specific to the corporation's industry.
- The corporation should begin to practice IT risk management by reviewing all systems for threats against security, privacy, and business interruptions.
- All contracts and insurance coverage should be reviewed for enforceable terms and sufficient coverages. Negotiate new contracts and obtain adequate coverage as needed.
- All IT marketing and sales materials need to be reviewed for promises and implied warranties that could prove troublesome should the company be sued for any product or service-related reason.
- IT marketing and sales materials should be redone to reflect the company's best-practice adherence.

The key to retrenchment activities is to view them as an opportunity to finish the work that was begun while solving the Y2K problem before new IT complexities engulf the organization. It may well be the last chance to get IT and its applications under corporate control instead of under the control of suppliers, vendors, and contractors who may not place a firm's best interests first. Now that the true nature and condition of the IT industry has been revealed and business's IT dependence clearly demonstrated, executives must take control of the situation and require that information technology serve the needs of business by demanding quality products and high-integrity service.

For the IT industry, the way to success is clearly marked for companies that can meet the challenge of quality and integrity, for they will be able to aid and not impede the successes of business in the next century.

Recommendation 16: Commission lessons-learned assessment of the corporation's Y2K experience identifying those IT management processes that were deficient. Plan an orderly return-to-the-basics initiative to bring IT processes to the level of industry best practices.

CLOSING WITH A CAUTIONARY NOTE

Following the year 2000, the pent-up demand for new software applications development and the implementation of web-based and e-commerce systems will be substantial. But the fact remains that most organizations have not yet solved all Y2K problems. In addition to any mission-critical system problems, there still exists the inventory of non–mission-critical systems needing remediation or replacement. Remaining systems to be corrected and brought to compliance will need to be subjected to the same process as the mission-critical systems, including full date testing. All of this work lies ahead through the early months of the year 2000. It is unrealistic for executive management to expect an immediate resumption of modernization efforts until all existing systems are compliant and stabilized.

Eventually, however, things will return to normal and the organization will be free to pursue new technologies and satisfy the pent-up demand of the business units. This book has aimed at assisting corporate executive management as they assume a greater role in the future management of IT and at convincing executives that future viability of the enterprise is directly dependent on how well IT is managed. While it took two missing digits and over 30 years to demonstrate the mismanagement of early system developments, continued mismanagement of IT will surface far more quickly in a world of on-line, web-based, and e-commerce applications. If a company utilizes the web or participates in e-commerce, that company, like it or not, is in the software business. The urgency with which IT and software must be brought under control can be demonstrated by reviewing the nature of risk in this new on-line world.

From a business perspective, several characteristics of web-based commerce reflect immediately on a company. For example, the personality and competence of a corporation is on display for all to see. Competition is just a mouse click away, and the impression projected by a web site substitutes for a salesperson. It is the goal of on-line commerce to induce a browser to become a buyer with all requisite actions carried out in the shortest conceivable time. To accomplish this, web-page and transaction design need to be crisp and clean. Ambiguity and clutter lead to buyer confusion, confusion may lead to questions, and questions lead to hesitation. Hesitation kills sales. In addition to effective page layouts to promote the product and clear ordering instructions, the entire operational configuration needs to perform to a high degree of reliability. To meet this specification, web-based business applications will need to overcome the following potential problems, thereby eliminating or reducing those unique risks associated with conducting on-line business. First, the application and configuration needs to be capable of continuous operation. Customers make purchases at any time of day—worldwide. This means that the operational complexity of the configuration and application will increase significantly over mainframe batch systems. From a configuration perspective, this means many redundancies throughout the local system and the network that ties your suppliers and delivery services together. Increasingly, the Internet serves the network function, but depending on confidentiality and integrity requirements, dedicated systems still may be needed to provide adequate security for the next few years.

In all cases, companies pursuing on-line commerce will need to evaluate the on-line competency of each other and their IT management track record.

Because of the interdependent nature of future on-line businesses, all partners will need to begin to manage IT according to best practices. Those that do will find partners; those that do not will not. There will develop a mutual policing of business partners so that all can benefit. To be included in the partnership, all who wish to participate in the realms of electronic business will be forced to adopt and enforce the best practices of IT management.

APPENDIX A

EXECUTIVES' GUIDE TO INFORMATION TECHNOLOGY METRICS

BACKGROUND: This guide provides the essential elements of data that should be captured by the managers of information technology (IT) in order to demonstrate control over operational computing assets, their ability to estimate project resource needs and set schedules, and for use in personnel performance evaluations.

While all of these measures are not necessary in every systems environment, executive management should require sufficient metrics gathering and reporting to feel comfortable that IT resources and projects are being controlled and monitored to a level commensurate with information technology's importance to the organization.

The metrics for 11 IT areas are presented. They cover comprehensive cost and workload categories used in many large IT operations. Whether the IT computing workload is being accomplished in-house or under contract, data concerning these categories are needed to properly manage IT finances and assets, production workloads, quality, telecommunications, customer service, systems under development, service-level agreements, and staffing.

The establishment and use of metrics is the most important first step in managing IT in the post–year 2000 world.

FINANCIAL METRICS: All data are gathered for a 12- to 18-month rolling period.

SUMMARY MEASURE	METRICS
Key Indicators	Expenses—Period Plan ($$$$$) Expenses—Period Actual ($$$$$) Staffing—Period Plan Staffing—Period Actual Computing Availability—Plan Computing Availability—Actual Billings—Plan ($$$$$) Billings—Actual ($$$$$)
Expense Performance Roll-up	Current Period—Plan ($$$$$) Current Period—Actual ($$$$$) Year to Date—Plan ($$$$$) Year to Date—Actual ($$$$$) YTD Variance from Plan—Period ($$$$$) YTD Variance from Plan—YTD ($$$$$)
Expense Variance by Cost Center	Current Period—Plan ($$$$$) Current Period—Actual ($$$$$) Current Period—Variance Analysis Cumulative YTD—Plan ($$$$$) Cumulative YTD—Actual ($$$$$) Cumulative YTD—Variance Analysis
Expense Variance by Category	Current Period—Plan ($$$$$) Current Period—Actual ($$$$$) Current Period—Variance Analysis Cumulative YTD—Plan ($$$$$) Cumulative YTD—Actual ($$$$$) Cumulative YTD—Variance Analysis
Performance Plan (Capital)	Current Period—Plan ($$$$$) Current Period—Actual ($$$$$) Year to Date—Plan ($$$$$) Year to Date—Actual ($$$$$) YTD Variance from Plan—Period ($$$$$) YTD Variance from Plan—YTD ($$$$$)
Billing Allocation	Current Period—Plan ($$$$$) Current Period—Actual ($$$$$)

FINANCIAL METRICS (Continued).

SUMMARY MEASURE	METRICS
Capital Expenditures (data captured for project life)	Project Capital—Year to Date ($$$$$) Project Capital—Inception to Date ($$$$$) Project Capital—Original Plan ($$$$$) Project Capital—Current Plan ($$$$$) Project Capital—Plan Variance ($$$$$)
System Usage by Customer (current fiscal year)	Current Period—Plan ($$$$$) Current Period—Actual ($$$$$)
Resource Usage by Customer (current fiscal year)	Usage Type—Development (%) Usage Type—Support (%) Usage Type—Storage (%) Usage Type—Processing (%) Usage Type—Communications (%) Usage Type—(%) of Total Available

STAFFING METRICS: All data are gathered for a 12- to 18-month rolling period.

SUMMARY MEASURE	METRICS

Staff Plan Performance	Employee Count—Actual vs. Plan
	    Actual Employees (Full-time Equivalent)
	    Contractors (Full-time Equivalent)
	Staffing Analysis
	    Actual Employees (Full-time Equivalent)
	    Contractors (Full-time Equivalent)

Employee Count Summary	Employees by Cost Center—Plan Employees by Cost Center—Actual Contractors by Cost Center—Plan Contractors by Cost Center—Actual Total by Job Series—Plan Total by Job Series—Actual Total by Cost Center—Plan Total by Cost Center—Actual
Employee Turnover Report	YTD Turnover by Department (%) YTD Turnover by Department (count) YTD Turnover by Job Series (%) YTD Turnover by Job Series (count)

COMPETITIVE COMPARISON: For IT Product and Service Companies

SUMMARY MEASURE	METRICS
IT Revenue & Capital	Expense as % of Revenue—Actual
	Expense as % of Revenue—Plan
	Expense per Customer—Actual ($$$$$)
	Expense per Customer—Plan ($$$$$)
	Capital as % of Revenue Actual
	Capital as % of Revenue Plan
IT Expenses & Staffing	IT Expenses vs. Company—3 Month Trend
	Actual (%)
	Plan (%)
	IT Staffing vs. Company—3 Month Trend
	Actual (%)
	Plan (%)
	IT Cost per Employee—3 Month Trend
	Actual ($$$$$)
	Plan ($$$$$)
Technology Insertion Trends	Number of Devices vs. Employees
	(over the last 18 months)

PRODUCTIVITY: All data are gathered for a 12- to 18-month period.

SUMMARY MEASURE	METRICS
System/Software Development Productivity	Units of Work Assigned—Plan (count)
	Units of Work Complete—Actual (count)
	Development Staffing—Actual # Full Time
	Development Staffing—Authorized
	Development Productivity Ratio
	Units of Work per Actual Full Time
	Units of Work Target
IT Production Support Productivity	# of Jobs Processed—Plan
	# of Jobs Processed—Actual
	Support Staffing—Actual # Full Time
	Support Staffing—Authorized
	Production Productivity Ratio
	Jobs Processed per Authorized
	Jobs Processed per Actual # Full Time
	Jobs Processed Target
Response Time Statistics	Application Response Time to User

SYSTEM/SOFTWARE DEVELOPMENT

SUMMARY MEASURE	METRICS
Service Request Backlog	# of Service Requests—Open # of Service Requests—Closed # of Service Requests—Backlog Backlog—Actual (estimated # of days) Backlog—Plan (estimated # of days) Time to Complete Priority 1 (days) Time to Complete Priority 2 (days) Time to Complete Priority 3 (days)
Project Status Reporting (data for life of project)	Detail Budget and Status by Approved Tasks 　Person-hours Approved 　Person-hours Actual 　Hours estimated to complete 　Person-hours total to complete 　Variance
Service Request Closure 　Priority 1	Service Requests Closed—Plan (count) Service Requests Closed—Actual (count)
Service Request Closure 　Priority 2 and 3	Service Requests Closed—Plan (count) Service Requests Closed—Actual (count)

LOCAL AREA NETWORK (LAN)—PCs: All data are gathered
for a 12- to 18-month period.

SUMMARY MEASURE	METRICS
LAN Performance	# of Service Work Orders—Plan (count)
	# of Service Work Orders—Actual (count)
	Cost of Service—Plan ($$$$$)
	Cost of Service—Actual ($$$$$)
	Cost per Service Order—Plan ($$$$$)
	Cost per Service Order—Actual ($$$$$)
LAN Project Status (data for life of project)	Detail Budget and Status by Approved Task
	Persons hours Approved
	Persons hours Actual
	Hours Estimated to Completed
	Person hours to Complete
	Variance

QUALITY ASSURANCE AND TESTING: All data are gathered
for a 12- to 18-month period.

SUMMARY MEASURE	METRICS
Development Reviews (walkthroughs, etc.)	# of Requirement Problems Discovered # of Design Flaws Discovered # of Standards Violations Discovered # of Program Errors before Testing
Test Results by Release	# of Defects Discovered by Testing 　# by Type 　# by Impact & Priority # of Defects Resolved & Retested 　# by Type 　# by Impact & Priority # of Defects Outstanding 　# by Type 　# by Impact & Priority
Release Test Comparison	(Note: These metrics show quality trends between different software/system releases.) Analysis of Problems in Prior Releases vs. the Current Release. 　# of Defects Discovered by Testing 　　# by Type 　　# by Impact & Priority 　# of Defects Resolved & Retested 　　# by Type 　　# by Impact & Priority 　# of Defects Outstanding 　　# by Type 　　# by Impact & Priority
Quality Improvement Efforts	Initial # of Defects by Type Current # of Defects by Type QA Plan Problems—Outstanding

CUSTOMER SERVICE/HELP DESK: All data are gathered
for a 12- to 18-month period.

SUMMARY MEASURE	METRICS
Workload Summary	Statistics—# of Incoming Calls Statistics—# of Outgoing Calls # of Problem Incidents Average # of Incidents per Operator
Quick-Fix Incidents	Quick-Fix Incidents—(count) Quick Fix—Fixed—(count) Quick-Fix Incident—Moving Average
Problem Notification Analysis	Problem by Source—Period (count) Problem by Source—YTD (count) Problem by User—Period (count) Problem by User—YTD (count)

Problem Notification by Priority	Number Reported:
	  Priority 1 (count)
	  Priority 2 (count)
	  Priority 3 (count)
	Number Closed:
	  Priority 1 (count)
	  Priority 2 (count)
	  Priority 3 (count)
	Number Unresolved:
	  Priority 1 (count)
	  Priority 2 (count)
	  Priority 3 (count)

Problem Notification by Category	Number Reported:
	  Hardware (count)
	  Communications/LAN (count)
	  Desktop (count)
	  Software (count)
	Number Closed:
	  Hardware (count)
	  Communications/LAN (count)
	  Desktop (count)
	  Software (count)

CUSTOMER SERVICE/HELP DESK (Continued)

SUMMARY MEASURE	METRICS
	Number Unresolved: Hardware (count) Communications/LAN (count) Desktop (count) Software (count)
Problem Closure Statistics	Priority 1—Days to Close—80% (average) Priority 1—Days to Close—All (average) Priority 1—Days to Close—Goal (average) Priority 2, 3—Days to Close—80% (average) Priority 2, 3—Days to Close—All (average) Priority 2, 3—Days to Close—Goal (average) Days to Close Trend: Priority 1 (3 month moving average) Priority 2 (3 month moving average) Priority 3 (3 month moving average)
Installation/Repair Management	PC/Terminal Installs—All (average days) PC/Terminal Installs—95% (average days) PC/Terminal Installs—Low (quickest days) PC/Terminal Installs—High (longest days) PC/Terminal Repair—All (average days) PC/Terminal Repair—95% (average days) PC/Terminal Repair—Low (quickest days) PC/Terminal Repair—High (longest days) Peripherals Installs—All (average days) Peripherals Installs—95% (average days) Peripherals Installs—Low (quickest days) Peripherals Installs—High (longest days) Peripherals Repair—All (average days) Peripherals Repair—95% (average days) Peripherals Repair—Low (quickest days) Peripherals Repair—High (longest days)

APPENDIX A

COMPUTER OPERATIONS: All data are gathered for a 12- to 18-month period. CPU = central processing unit. MIPS = million instructions per second. DASD = direct access storage device.

SUMMARY MEASURE	METRICS
Computer Capacity	CPU Usage—MIPS Peak (number)
	CPU Usage—MIPS Average (number)
	CPU Usage—Maximum (number)
	CPU Usage—Acceptable (number)
	DASD Usage—Gigabytes—Maximum
	DASD Usage—Gigabytes—Actual (usage)
Computer Workload Throughput	CPU On-line Transactions—Plan (count)
	CPU On-line Transactions—Actual (count)
	Batch Production Jobs—Plan (count)
	Batch Production Jobs—Actual (count)
On-line Performance Summary	On-line Availability—Plan (%)
	On-line Availability—Actual (%)
	On-line Response Time—Plan (seconds)
	On-line Response Time—Average (seconds)
	On-line Response Time—90% (seconds)
Computer Outages	Number of Outages (count)
	Total Outage Time (minutes)
	Average Resolution Time—Goal (minutes)
	Average Resolution Time—Average (min.)
	Mean Time Between Failure—(minutes)
Batch Performance Summary	Batch Performance—On Time %-Plan
	Batch Performance—On Time %-Actual
Report Distribution and Billing Performance	Reports Delivered On Time %-Plan
	Reports Delivered On Time %-Actual
	Billing Performance—Days Early/Late Actual
	Billing Performance—Days Early/Late Plan
System Resource Chargeback	Billings for Resources Usage by Department YTD (percent)

COMMUNICATIONS: All data are gathered for a 12- to 18-month period.

SUMMARY MEASURE	METRICS
Network Outages	Number of Network Outages (count) Total Outage Time (minutes) Average Resolution Time—Goal (minutes) Average Resolution Time—Average (minutes)
Switch Performance Statistics Internet Billings	Number of Trunks Busy—Plan (count) Number of Trunks Busy—Actual (count) Internet Provider Billings—Actual ($$$$$) Internet Provider Billings—Plan ($$$$$)
Voice Mail Performance	Number of Users—Plan (count) Number of Users—Actual (count)
LAN Analysis	Number of Users—Plan (count) Number of Users—Actual (count) Software Licenses—Number ($$$$$) Server Capacity—Plan—Gigabytes Server Capacity—Actual Used—Gigabytes
PC/Workstation Analysis	Number of PC/Workstations—Plan (count) Number of PC/Workstations—Actual (count) Utilization by Department—Plan (%) Utilization by Department—Actual (%)

APPENDIX B

SYSTEMS DEVELOPMENT PROCESS FRAMEWORK

This framework presents for executive management an easy-to-use guide for exercising IT project oversight and for monitoring systems development progress. It is comprised of two parts: the life-cycle phases of an IT project and the several management requirement plans that ensure project success. The framework can be viewed as a matrix of cells by extending the horizontal lines separating the phases across the form. Executives need to be aware that distinct actions need to be accomplished in each cell for each management requirement plan at each phase of the life cycle. This framework presents the life-cycle phases and management requirement plans that are generally included as industry best practices. Progression down the phases should be uniform with no one management requirement plan getting too far ahead or behind the other plans.

To aid executive management in their oversight role, this appendix provides a short description of each life-cycle phase and presents key questions to ask concerning each management requirement plan as an IT project progresses.

LIFE-CYCLE PHASES

These phases identify discrete steps in a systems development or systems integration project. Each phase produces distinct work products resulting from analysis performed during that phase. A project should not progress from one phase to the next until all work products are completed or accounted for.

PREPARATION PHASE

This phase requires that overall project definition and scope be determined to the extent that initial budgets and resource estimates can be formulated. Each management requirement category should be examined for applicability to the project being considered and initial plan outlines developed. Each management requirement needs to be planned or waived with justification. The hardware, software, and network infrastructure needed to operate the finished system should be documented, if known. The project concept should be submitted to a full feasibility study and an initial risk assessment.

DEFINITION PHASE

This phase proceeds with detailed definition of the business requirement and associated technology support requirements. A determination is made concerning the most feasible solution from among the alternatives submitted to the feasibility study. Each management plan determined to be appropriate for this project defines its unique set of requirements dictated by the business application and the selected technical solution to be developed or integrated throughout the rest of the project's life cycle. Each management plan, by the end of this phase, will have a documented list of project requirements that will need to be satisfied before the overall development project can be considered complete. Some of the requirements deal with business aspects of the system, some deal with quality characteristics of the system, while others address security and internal control issues.

DESIGN PHASE

This phase is involved with designing a technical and human factors solution to the business problem or opportunity while satisfying the requirements imposed by applicable management plans. For virtually all systems, the design will have to address security, internal controls, and documentation requirements. Software or systems engineering plans ensure that the design and subsequent development adhere to proven structured software engineering techniques. To ensure a quality system and one that can be maintained over its projected life, other management plans are used to guide the development or integration activities of quality assurance and testing, technology transfer to customers, and training. All plans confirm to standards prescribed in the project management plan by the project manager. Business unit stakeholders and corporate legal, audit, and security staffs should concur on designs and project plans.

DEVELOPMENT PHASE

This phase converts the business and technology systems design into an automated system as modified by the security and internal controls design and human factors. It may require original software programming and database development or, more commonly, the integration of various products into an operational system that performs the business function. During development the quality assurance and testing plan and the configuration management plan take on great importance as the activities that oversee development to ensure project/system/product/service integrity.

DEPLOYMENT

Upon completion of development and following customer/user accept-ance of the system or integration, this phase addresses the fielding of the system for operational business use or for sale. For any deployment to be successful, all applicable management requirement plans must have been completed through the end of the development phase. Actions not com-pleted means the system/product/service is not yet ready for introduction to the marketplace or workplace. Phased deployments are common with large distributed systems of great hardware and network complexity. Phased software deployments where incomplete functionality is released for use should be considered incomplete projects and highly risky. At the end of deployment, all business, technical, and management requirements need to have been completed, fully tested, and documented.

MAINTENANCE

This final phase requires the accurate completion and currency of all sys-tems documentation, vendor products, and networks in order to be able to modify, enhance, or correct defects in the deployed system in a timely fash-ion. Expect this phase to consume an inordinate amount of resources if the system is not developed according to best practices.

INSTRUCTIONS FOR USE

Executives may utilize the framework in an active or passive manner. First, it may be necessary to impose the framework on the system developers and contractors of an organization if they do not employ one of their own choosing. If this is the case, the problems facing the IT group probably are far greater than can be solved just by requiring the use of a systems devel-opment model. It is hoped that senior executives have some form of IT organizational structure to work through, in such case, a less direct approach will suffice. A more passive implementation would be simply to use the framework and the questions in each of the management require-ment plan areas as a "crib sheet" to guide progress reviews. Much depends on management style.

B.1 SYSTEMS DEVELOPMENT PROCESS FRAMEWORK

MANAGEMENT REQUIREMENTS

Life-Cycle Phases	Project Management Plan	Software Engineering Plan	Internal Controls Plan	Security Plan	QA & Testing Plan	CM Plan	Documentation Plan	Technology Transfer Plan	Training Plan	Infrastructure Risk Monitoring		
										Hardware	Software	Network
Preparation												
Definition												
Design												
Development												
Deployment												
Maintenance												

186

B.2 PROJECT MANAGEMENT PLAN

Life-Cycle Phases	MANAGEMENT REQUIREMENTS		
	PROJECT MANAGEMENT PLAN: This plan is the control point for project planning, budgeting, resource management, risk management, and technical reviews. This plan should adhere to a corporate standard for project management. A business unit executive should be named sponsor for the project before work begins.		
Preparation	• Have all actions to make this an approved corporate work project been completed? • Have initial draft budgets been prepared with input from business units and other stakeholders? • Has a full feasibility study been performed? If not, why not? Has an initially feasible solution been determined? • Has an initial security and project risk assessment been conducted?		
Definition	• Have all business units and stakeholders defined their respective requirements for this system? • Are all requirements associated with an approved business function or corporate management need? • Does the completed definition of requirements have the approval of the security, legal, and audit staffs?		
Design	• Have all requirements been accepted and approved by the appropriate business unit before detailed design begins? • Is a structured design methodology being followed? If not, why not? • Has the initial risk assessment been updated? Is the solution in design still feasible?		
Development	• Has the system's design been approved by the appropriate business unit? Have workplace issues been included? • Are quality assurance procedures being followed during programming? Are structured tests being conducted? • Are all necessary hardware, software, and network acquisitions under way and on schedule?		
Deployment	• Have all systems, including package software, completed integration testing before deployment? • Have all support hardware, software, and network modifications been installed and checked out? • Have systems passed user acceptance testing? • Are all documentation and training materials complete? Have all user acceptance signatures been obtained?		
Maintenance	• Is staffing sufficient and prepared to conduct maintenance on the system? • Is change control in place and being enforced? • Are security and internal controls being monitored according to security policy? Is intrusion detection in place?		

B.3 SOFTWARE ENGINEERING PLAN

Life-Cycle Phases	MANAGEMENT REQUIREMENTS
	SOFTWARE ENGINEERING PLAN: This plan concentrates on the structured software engineering methods to be followed when creating the software system or integrating off-the-shelf packages and system components. This plan enforces structured methods throughout the development as an IT best practice.
Preparation	• Has a structured software development and/or integration methodology been selected? Is it sufficient to the task? • From a staffing perspective, can the IT organization support the methodology; or will contractors be required? • Do automated tools, software packages, or additional hardware need to be acquired to support the project?
Definition	• Are users and other stakeholders prepared to interface with the development team in use of the methodology? • Does the engineering methodology capture and document all requirements needed for this development? • Have all business requirements and management plan requirements been captured according to the methodology? • Have all requirements been approved by appropriate managers? Have risk assessments been updated?
Design	• Are "logical" models of the system being developed to record the design? Are all data elements standardized and recorded? Are "logical" models updated as changes in design occur? • Do quality assurance reviews occur periodically? Is the design under configuration management? • Have all system requirements been satisfied by the design? Do all stakeholders concur?
Development	• Do programming and/or integration specifications exist? Do they reflect the design? Have they been reviewed for quality? • Are code inspections being conducted? Are technology transfer and training materials being prepared? • Has unit, system, and integration testing been completed? Have all tests and test materials been documented? • Are all code, data, tests, and test materials under configuration management?
Deployment	• Are documentation requirements satisfied? • Are supporting hardware, software packages, and networks ready for deployment? • Have end-to-end system tests with business partners been completed? Have users accepted the system?
Maintenance	• Are requests for system modification submitted for impact analysis? • Are approved changes under change control and configuration management? • Is all systems documentation up to date?

B.4 INTERNAL CONTROLS PLAN

Life-Cycle Phases	MANAGEMENT REQUIREMENTS		
	INTERNAL CONTROLS PLAN: This plan focuses attention on the need for the system under development to satisfy the legal, accounting, and data consistency requirements of the corporation, the corporation's industry, and regulators. The American Institute of Certified Public Accountants (AICPA) prescribes such rules as does the company's external auditor.		
Preparation	• Have pertinent legal, accounting, audit, and internal control requirements been identified? Have stakeholders to these requirements been alerted to the need for their assistance in determining those requirements? • Are all regulatory reporting requirements known? Does this effort require a special legal review?		
Definition	• Have accountant and auditor stakeholders participated in defining comprehensive system requirements? If not, why not? • Have specific internal controls and audit trails been proposed that are adequate to identified risks and to meet regulatory requirements? • Are specific tests and test data for internal controls being defined? Are system success criteria known?		
Design	• Do "logical" design models of the system reflect the presence of internal controls and audit trails? Are specific data and processing "consistency" checks designed into the system? • Have the design of internal controls been reviewed, and are they deemed adequate by an external auditor? • Have test materials for internal controls been independently reviewed and verified as sufficient to verify the controls?		
Development	• Have internal control and consistency checks been included in programming specifications before coding begins? • Are internal control and consistency checks under configuration management? • Are all controls and consistency checks being included in program and systems testing?		
Deployment	• Have accounting and auditor stakeholders approved the code implementation of specified internal controls and checks? • Are programmed controls adequately documented to facilitate efficient use by auditors during systems operations? • Are user documents and training clear about internal controls and user interface during the systems operation?		
Maintenance	• Are routine system modifications reviewed for impact on internal controls and consistency checks? • Are controls periodically tested to ensure continued reliability and to uncover possible tampering with the controls? • Are all controls documented and kept current under CM?		

Life-Cycle Phases	MANAGEMENT REQUIREMENTS		
	SECURITY PLAN: This plan ensures that security, confidentiality, integrity, and system availability/reliability features are designed into the system under development and are integral to its operation. This is opposed to the piecemeal approach of adding security features onto a system, with little or no analysis, as it nears completion.		
Preparation	• Have all pertinent security and data confidentiality requirements been identified? Is a security risk analysis required by statute, regulation, or industry standard practice? What availability/reliability levels are needed to support the business? • Are security stakeholders involved in this development or integration project? If not, why not? Is legal reviewing for security issues? Have any security models or standards been identified that should guide this effort?		
Definition	• Has a formal threat assessment been performed to uncover technical and business risks associated with this system? • Has security been included in the project's budget? Are business continuity plans being developed for the system? • Are security control specifications included in the approved statement of system requirement? Do stakeholders concur?		
Design	• Do "logical" design models include security features? Are database controls being designed? • Are design reviews examining security features? Is an independent group reviewing the design for security adequacy? • Are security feature tests being prepared? Are success criteria for these tests known?		
Development	• Are security controls being integrated into system's program code and documentation? • Are security controls and security documentation under configuration management? • Are third-party software packages being researched and/or tested for security features and reliability?		
Deployment	• Have all security test results been reviewed and approved by security stakeholders? • Are security features still accurately documented? • Do operating instructions reflect security? Is training in security controls complete?		
Maintenance	• Are all system changes reviewed for their impact on security and system availability/reliability? • Are all system modifications tested for security rule adherence and for negative security impact? • Are all security documents up to date and under configuration management?		

B.6 QUALITY ASSURANCE & TESTING PLAN

Life-Cycle Phases	MANAGEMENT REQUIREMENTS		
	QUALITY ASSURANCE (QA) & TESTING PLAN: This plan prescribes the quality certifications required of the finished software or system. The International Standards Organization (ISO-9000) and American National Standards Institute (ANSI) series guide quality efforts and are required by many customers. System criticality and information sensitivity determine the degree of testing that is appropriate and demonstrates that "reasonable care" was exercised in the development of the system.		
Preparation	• Have quality standards for this development been determined? • Have ISO-9000, ANSI, and/or industry-specific standards been selected to guide the project's quality assurance effort? • Has an independent validation and verification been deemed advisable?		
Definition	• Have all quality characteristics for the system under development been defined and specified (i.e., accuracy, timeliness, etc.)? • Are the quality characteristics measurable and therefore testable? • Is each quality characteristic and its measurement criteria fully documented as a requirement?		
Design	• Are periodic quality reviews scheduled to ensure that "structured" methods are being adhered to by the developers? • When discovered, are design defects being recorded, resolved, and entered into a QA metrics database? • Are test cases and test data being designed by the QA group as the system is being designed?		
Development	• Are documentation and code reviews being conducted independent of the original programmer? • Is unit, program, and systems testing being conducted? • Are coding and other defects being recorded, resolved, and entered into the QA metrics database?		
Deployment	• Are system integration and workplace acceptance tests being conducted? Are performance tests being conducted? • Has all development and testing documentation been through a quality review? • Are all test cases and other test materials finalized before system release to production status?		
Maintenance	• Do quality reviews continue for all changes to the production system? • Are test cases and other test materials under configuration management? • Is all documentation up to date?		

B.7 CONFIGURATION MANAGEMENT

Life-Cycle Phases	MANAGEMENT REQUIREMENTS
	CONFIGURATION MANAGEMENT (CM): This is a project control plan that focuses on the identification and management of work products, or "artifacts," being produced by the development effort. The plan defines how an inventory of all work products (i.e. requirements, designs, code, tests, and documents) will be recorded and accurately maintained for the life of the system. Without CM, work products cannot be monitored properly and confusion results.
Preparation	• Has a CM process been defined for this project? Is it consistent with best practices and corporate policy? Will CM be accomplished manually or using automated tools? Will CM-trained employees be ready on the first day of the project? • Has an individual empowered to enforce CM been identified? Does the person independently report to the project manager? • Does the person monitoring CM have the authority to stop project activities until CM deficiencies are resolved?
Definition	• Do all participants on the project understand the CM process to be used? Is training in automated CM tools complete? • Upon completion of the definition phase, are all requirements identified and under configuration management before proceeding with system design? Are all changes to requirements being reviewed for overall impact on the project?
Design	• Are all work products from the design being placed under CM? • Are changes to the design being properly brought under CM? Are changes being evaluated for overall impact on the design? • Have test cases and test materials been brought under CM? Are documentation and training materials under CM? • Does the person monitoring CM report to the project manager any deviation from CM policy or process?
Development	• Is all programming documentation and code under CM? Have any audits of the CM process and the daily baseline been conducted? Do all program changes undergo an impact analysis to determine effect on the system? • Are all test materials remaining under CM? Are all documentation and training materials still under enforced CM?
Deployment	• Are all system documents, code, reports, testing, and training materials under CM, in their final form, before release of the system for production or for sale? Are all baselines final?
Maintenance	• Are all system documents, code, reports, testing, and operations materials maintained under CM consistently updated to reflect the production system accurately? Have any audits been performed to confirm this?

192

B.8 DOCUMENTATION PLAN

Life-Cycle Phases	MANAGEMENT REQUIREMENTS
	DOCUMENTATION PLAN: This plan concentrates on producing sufficient and comprehensible documentation that accurately depicts the work products of all developmental actions that occur in each life-cycle phase such that each document guides the work to be done in subsequent phases.
Preparation	• Have all system-level and business-level documentation requirements been identified? Have all legal, regulatory, and best-practice documentation requirements been identified? Has documentation production during systems development and the maintenance of such documents over the anticipated life of the system been budgeted?
Definition	• Are system requirements being documented in a manner that will facilitate future changes and maintenance by people not involved in the original development effort? • Will human factors be considered in the development of documents and their presentation to employees or customers? • Have documentation requirements been reviewed for comprehensiveness and clarity of purpose?
Design	• Are system design documents being generated using one of the best-practice structured approaches? • Are system test design documents complete? • Are all documents complete and have they been reviewed for quality and clarity? • Are all documents under configuration management (CM)?
Development	• Are program flows being documented so that system interfaces and inputs and outputs are clear and understandable? • Is all programming logic being documented? Are databases and their structure documented? • Are all test plans and test data fully documented so that they can be utilized again for the life of the system? • Is there, under CM, an accurate daily baseline of all programming, database, and testing documentation?
Deployment	• Is all finalized documentation printed or available electronically to all users or customers before release of the system? • Are all final documents, in whatever media, under CM, and do they accurately reflect all other work products under CM?
Maintenance	• Are system and user documents kept current reflecting changes to the system or to workplace operating procedures? • Are test materials and documents kept up to date?

B.9 TECHNOLOGY TRANSFER PLAN

Life-Cycle Phases	Management Requirements		
	TECHNOLOGY TRANSFER PLAN: This plan ensures that "new" technology and features of the "new" system are thoroughly understood by employees/customers who must use and maintain them. This is true even if the system's operation is to be outsourced. Usability, maintainability, and sustainability are the objectives of this plan.		
Preparation	• Is the system's proposed technology consistent with approved corporate standards? Are new standards needed? Have the issues of usability, maintainability, and sustainability been evaluated during the feasibility study? • Should a "pilot" project for this "new" technology be considered?		
Definition	• Have all technical interfaces and sociotechnical interactions been identified for this system? • Are workplace procedural changes needed? Who will modify those procedures? Have necessary employee/customer skills for training been identified? Have technology transfer activities been funded? Are any acquisitions required?		
Design	• Has a strategy for the transfer of technology from developers/contractors to user/employees been developed? • Has a strategy for the transfer of systems from developers/contractors to system maintainers been developed? • Has each strategy been funded?		
Development	• Has the technology transfer strategy been approved by all stakeholders to the project? • Are all system design and development work products ready for transfer? • Have acquisitions to support the transfer of technology been completed? Are site surveys and transfer plans required?		
Deployment	• Are all physical office locations ready for the insertion of the technology? • Are early deployments being audited to obtain feedback that may influence the remainder of the deployments? • Are all management requirement categories completed prior to full fielding of the system?		
Maintenance	• Have all elements of the system needed for effective and efficient maintenance been turned over to maintenance personnel? • Have operations and maintenance personnel accepted responsibility for the system? • Are support contracts with suppliers in place?		

Life-Cycle Phases	MANAGEMENT REQUIREMENTS		
	TRAINING PLAN: This plan directs the identification, preparation, and dissemination of training and instructional materials needed for the successful deployment, use, maintenance, and operation of the final developed system. This includes modified workplace procedures and forms for use by employees.		
Preparation	• Do mandated training requirements exist? Are there industry-related standards for instructional or training materials? • What are competitors providing their customers or employees? Is professional training contractor support needed? • Is training included in the initial budget projection?		
Definition	• Are criteria to ensure successful learning being incorporated into the specifications for technical training materials? • Does the company have the expertise to do this? • Have the training's presentation media been determined and included in the project's budget?		
Design	• Are training materials being designed concurrent with the design of the system? Does the system's design team include instructional design experience? • Do supporting contractor's training design and presentation abilities meet professional standards?		
Development	• Are training materials being prepared as systems near completion of programming and testing? • Are training materials in agreement with actual design and programming documentation? Do training materials reflect how the system really will work? Are anticipated error conditions and resolution procedures included in the training? • Have training materials been reviewed independently by the business units implementing the system?		
Deployment	• Are training materials being evaluated as part of scheduled pilot projects before full deployment? • Have training materials been completed and checked for quality before full deployment of the system or before sale?		
Maintenance	• Are training and other instructional materials updated as system changes occur? • Are training and instructional materials kept under configuration management?		

B.11 INFRASTRUCTURE AND RISK MONITORING

Life-Cycle Phases	MANAGEMENT REQUIREMENTS	Infrastructure and Risk Monitoring		
		Hardware	Software	Networks
	INFRASTRUCTURE AND RISK MONITORING: As part of a systems development or systems integration effort, this activity monitors all other Management Requirement Plans and the hardware, software, and network support infrastructure for risks that may adversely effect the success of the project. This focus on risk management is done in conjunction with Appendix C.			
Preparation	• What risks, identified during previous projects, may pertain to this development or integration effort? • Are processing support infrastructures stable and sufficient for this effort or must new hardware, software, and networks be acquired and implemented? Are these acquisitions budgeted?			
Definition	• Have risks, identified during the feasibility study, a formal risk analysis, or through use of Appendix C, been factored into this project's plans? Has a mechanism to monitor these risks been determined? • Have mitigation plans for unresolved risks been development for later use if need be?			
Design	• Are system designs being reviewed for risks to information security, processing integrity, and customer acceptability? Is the need for this system still valid? • Is the development schedule still valid? Is the budget still sufficient? • Are all Management Requirement demands being satisfied or is the project at risk due to lack of SDP enforcement?			
Development	• Are all development work products in synch and fully documented? Are project work products under CM? • Are contractors delivering according to their statement of work? • Have identified security and integrity risks been addressed during development? Are they fully tested and documented?			
Deployment	• Have necessary infrastructure upgrades been received, installed and tested to determine their stability? • Are employees prepared to operate and maintain the system? Is the workplace ready? Is the product ready for sale? • Have support vendors and/or business partners delivered according to plan?			
Maintenance	• Are all the Management Requirements needed for systems operation and maintenance complete? • Have any necessary risk mitigation changes been fully incorporated into the final system? • Are Disaster Recovery and Business Continuity Plans in place and tested? Will they be updated as changes occur?			

APPENDIX C

RISK MANAGEMENT REVIEW MODEL

INSTRUCTIONS FOR USE

The information technology risk management review model provides executive management with the ability to monitor several categories of information technology project and operational risk that often are overlooked by the IT staff and even the business unit due to their focus on the technology of the system under development.

The risk areas suggested in this appendix require access to information that commonly goes beyond the purview of the technology staff. Thus, other corporate staff groups as necessary must be involved to ensure that all risk areas are addressed adequately.

The areas being recommended for special executive oversight include the following. (See pages 92–104 for a discussion of each risk area.)

- Failure of underlying technology
- Likelihood of support vendor failure
- Likelihood that employee marketplace can support the technology
- Likelihood of losing competitive advantage due to project delays
- Risk of creeping requirements
- Risks posed by emerging liability challenge
- Risks based on meaningless warranties
- Likelihood of new laws and regulations governing IT
- Continuing risk of IT project delay, abandonment, and marginal success

The methodology best used to determine these risks and to assess their impact is the "Delphi" approach where individuals and outside experts who are monitoring the various potential risks are polled as to impact. A consensus is reached and appropriate action is taken.

From time to time, other risk areas may be identified as being in need of executive monitoring. The executive IT management committee chaired by the CEO is the appropriate place to periodically review the risks covered by this appendix.

IT Risk Management Review

RISK AREA 1:	Failure of an Underlying Technology

Original Need
or Opportunity for
this Project: _____

Change Summary: _____

Change Summary: _____

Change Summary: _____

Impact on Project: _____

Dollar Change:
Impact on Project: _____

Dollar Change:
Mitigating Actions: _____

Continued
Project Viability: _____

RISK AREA 2:	Likelihood of Support Vendor Failure

Original Need
or Opportunity for
this Project:
_____

Change Summary:
_____

Change Summary:
_____

Change Summary:
_____

Impact on Project:
_____

Dollar Change:
Impact on Project:
_____

Dollar Change:
Mitigating Actions:
_____

Continued
Project Viability:
_____

RISK AREA 3:   Likelihood that Employee Marketplace Can Support
the Technology

Original Need
or Opportunity for _____
this Project: _____

Change Summary: _____
_____
_____

Change Summary: _____
_____
_____

Change Summary: _____
_____
_____

Impact on Project: _____
_____

Dollar Change: _____
Impact on Project: _____
_____

Dollar Change: _____
Mitigating Actions: _____
_____
_____

Continued _____
Project Viability: _____
_____

RISK AREA 4:   Likelihood of Losing Competitive Advantage
Due to Project Delays

Original Need
or Opportunity for   _____
this Project: _____

Change Summary: _____
_____
_____

Change Summary: _____
_____
_____

Change Summary: _____
_____
_____

Impact on Project: _____
_____

Dollar Change:
Impact on Project: _____
_____

Dollar Change:
Mitigating Actions: _____
_____
_____

Continued
Project Viability: _____
_____

APPENDIX C

RISK AREA 5:	Risk of Creeping Requirements

Original Need
or Opportunity for
this Project: _____

Change Summary: _____

Change Summary: _____

Change Summary: _____

Impact on Project: _____

Dollar Change:
Impact on Project: _____

Dollar Change:
Mitigating Actions: _____

Continued
Project Viability: _____

RISK AREA 6:   Risk Posed by Emerging Liability Challenge

Original Need
or Opportunity for
this Project:

Change Summary:

Change Summary:

Change Summary:

Impact on Project:

Dollar Change:
Impact on Project:

Dollar Change:
Mitigating Actions:

Continued
Project Viability:

APPENDIX C

RISK AREA 7:	Risk Posed by Meaningless Warranties

Original Need
or Opportunity for
this Project:

Change Summary:

Change Summary:

Change Summary:

Impact on Project:

Dollar Change:
Impact on Project:

Dollar Change:
Mitigating Actions:

Continued
Project Viability:

APPENDIX C

RISK AREA 8:	Likelihood of New Laws and Regulations Governing IT

Original Need
or Opportunity for
this Project: _____

Change Summary: _____

Change Summary: _____

Change Summary: _____

Impact on Project: _____

Dollar Change:
Impact on Project: _____

Dollar Change:
Mitigating Actions: _____

Continued
Project Viability: _____

207

RISK AREA 9:	Continuing Risk of IT Project Delay, Abandonment, and Marginal Success

Original Need
or Opportunity for _____
this Project: _____

Change Summary: _____
_____
_____

Change Summary: _____
_____
_____

Change Summary: _____
_____
_____

Impact on Project: _____
_____

Dollar Change: _____
Impact on Project: _____
_____

Dollar Change: _____
Mitigating Actions: _____
_____
_____

Continued _____
Project Viability: _____
_____

_____ APPENDIX D _____

EXECUTIVES NEED
TO PREPARE FOR THE
SYSTEMS-RELATED
LIABILITY CHALLENGE

In the aftermath of Y2K, software and systems liability cases before the court will force a rethinking of the conditions under which software developers can be held responsible and accountable for the quality (i.e., integrity and reliability) of the software and systems they develop and market. Likewise, organizations that are reliant on software and systems in the conduct of business will have their responsibilities to customers and third parties, for the reliability of their products or services, reexamined. Even though safe haven legislation was passed, giving broad protection to software vendors and companies for Y2K failures, it may actually result in a backlash against software vendors for all other types of defects in software that consumers heretofore have patiently accepted.

This discussion anticipates evolving legal thinking concerning the issues of software and systems liability. It presents a series of questions, with narrative, concerning actions that systems developers and business users should consider taking to decrease the likelihood of a successful legal action being brought against them. In anticipating possible post–year 2000 leanings of the courts, use of these questions can help determine the reasonableness of software and systems development procedures and/or system use management practices. They can serve as an indicator of possible problems requiring corrective action. As an added bonus, these same questions and subsequent actions can improve the overall quality of software and/or improve a company's use of IT and subsequent competitiveness in the marketplace.

PERCEPTIONS CONCERNING SOFTWARE AND ITS USES ARE MOST IMPORTANT

Often it is the perceived, as well as the actual, lack of software and systems quality that results in legal entanglements. Software, and the business use of software, has many characteristics. Successful use is judged by how well the following quality attributes are satisfied. Does the software, in its business use, exhibit the necessary degree of: correctness, usability, reliability, integrity, and confidentiality. Is the software and the subsequent business process maintainable, auditable, and well documented? Does it operate efficiently and satisfy the company's end customer?

Again, such terms are commonly used to describe characteristics of software, systems performance, and business outputs generated by the execution of the software. When these characteristic terms, however measured, are not satisfied, quality is seen to be lacking. If businesses or individuals believe they have suffered because of this lack of quality, legal action is a distinct possibility.

EVOLVING THEORIES OF RESPONSIBILITY

While certain contracting arrangements and disclaimer language can reduce liability, it must be recognized that these contracts and clauses work in some cases and are useless in others. Successful arguments have been made that contracts and disclaimer clauses can be ignored altogether in cases where a flawed computer system or software program results in personal catastrophe. This argument falls under the category of negligence and is not based on any kind of contract. The question that is posed is simple: Did the company do anything or fail to do anything that caused harm to someone else? If so, the company can be held liable for that harm. This is based on the legal theory that companies owe customers a certain minimal "duty of care." But against what standard will duty of care be measured? For the individual programmer, the question of being held to a "professional standard" is being openly debated at this time. Some hold that programmers lack full recognition as professionals in the same sense as doctors, lawyers, and accountants, and therefore seem safe from malpractice suits. Others believe that the code of ethics that members of various information technology associations and societies subscribe to opens analysts and programmers to potential lawsuits as professionals or at the very least highly trained experts. If so, analysts and programmers might find themselves in much the same position as accountants for whom there are established precedents as to their liability.

The courts may establish another possible standard, that of considering a computer program to be an inherently dangerous instrument, as in the case of air traffic control, nuclear plants, or medical device systems. Such a standard, if established, would require the greatest possible degree of care in the construction and use of the software and its business system implementations.

There is also the legal catchall of strict liability. This is the foundation of the product liability suit. This rationale holds that if a company makes a product, it is in a better position than anyone else to anticipate and reduce any hazard. Under strict liability, the company is expected to warn customers of any such remaining hazard. There is legal precedent for imposing liability for defective design, and a faulty program could easily be shown to be the result of a bad design.

Regardless of how the legal arguments are resolved, there will no doubt be an impact on organizations that design and development software systems and those that use automation in the pursuit of their business objectives. Undoubtedly one of the impacts will center on the methods and practices used to construct computer programs and implement those programs in business work processes. It is not clear at this time how the courts will determine which methods, techniques, and practices analysts and programmers should or should not have used in the design and coding of software and in the implementation of a business work process. The courts probably will hear testimony by computer experts and decide whether the analyst and programmer did what those of similar education, skill, and experience would have done with a similar set of business requirements. And the courts undoubtedly will look at the issue of whether the programmer adequately tested the program and system and adequately warned the user, or his or her manager, of the program's limitations.

Of course, from a practical perspective, the "analyst and programmer" being referred to in discussions of this sort are not individuals, except in the case of the independent consultant or "moonlighter," but the many analysts, designers, programmers, testers, documentors, and managers who collectively construct software and systems within a corporate structure and according to its corporate policies and practices. These are the policies and practices that will be called into question when a liability suit is directed against a company; not the knowledge, skills, and work habits of individuals acting without supervision and in isolation—unless of course, one is willing to admit that analysts and programmers working on corporate or client projects work in isolation and without supervision.

LIKELY SCENARIOS

Developers of software and systems or implementors and users of business processes dependent on software and systems might have to face any one of the following situations: After Y2K, the distinction between the two is going to blur.

- Software, system, or business process fails and the company is sued.

- Software, system, or business process is *not* the cause of a failure but the firm is sued anyway.

- Managers are asked to give the board of directors assurances that the corporation is producing quality software and systems, or is implementing quality business processes and could successfully defend against a lawsuit.

HOW MIGHT A LIABILITY CASE UNFOLD?

At the center of a plaintiff's strategy to win a liability case is the need to prove that development of the software/system in question did not meet accepted industry best practices necessary to demonstrate that reasonable care was exercised. *Black's Law Dictionary* defines reasonable care as "that degree of care which a person of ordinary prudence would exercise in the same or similar circumstances." Put another way, the developer did not exercise due diligence, defined by the *Plain Language Law Dictionary* as "the degree of effort and care in carrying out an act or obligation that the average, sincere, energetic person would exhibit," also "conduct that is devoid of negligence or carelessness."

To satisfy these definitions, it must be shown that there exists a standard body of knowledge and practice concerning the development of software and systems that is widely subscribed to by the industry, taught at the university, and used as the generally accepted method of planning, designing, programming, delivering, operating, and maintaining software and systems. It must be shown that this "standard" way of doing business is recognized by system and software developers as the recommended way to conduct a development effort in order to deliver the best possible product to their customer.

Such a de facto standard does exist and is commonly referred to as a systems or software development process (SDP). The SDP is the systematic and analytic process by which:

- Software and system development efforts are planned and managed

- Requirements are defined, analyzed, and specified

- Solutions are evaluated and determined to be feasible

- Solutions are designed to meet specified requirements
- Programs are coded and tested, databases built, equipments selected
- System components are assembled and tested together
- All development is documented and maintained
- Software and systems are accepted by the customer

There are many variations of the SDP. Some have very strict methodologies and are supported by automated tools. Some are more flexible and promote concurrent execution of certain development steps. Most versions of the SDP are designed to impose discipline on the business of programming software and systems. Any of the industry-accepted variations of the SDP are valid if they follow the proven steps of problem solving. But, in the rush to get to get someone coding, all SDPs tend to be ignored, circumvented, or applied incompletely.

A classic cartoon says it best. The supervisor is pictured about to leave a room of computer programmers. His instructions, "you all begin programming, I'll go see what they want." In other words, start building a solution before we have even defined the problem. An insider joke among systems people is the fact that they all admit to having some form of SDP to follow when doing their work. The insider also will readily admit that they do not, for whatever reason, use, or enforce the use of the SDP. This is like a surgeon failing to follow standard operating procedures when performing an appendectomy.

Again, the question to be asked will be quite simple: Did the company do anything or fail to do anything that caused harm? If it failed to follow the recognized industry practice for developing software and systems, perhaps it did not provide the plaintiff with the degree of "reasonable care" that was needed given the potential for harm. If developers did not avail themselves of the discipline of the SDP, it may even be difficult to claim that they knew what the potential for harm was so that special precautions such as an increase in testing, could be taken during development. Yes, bugs occur and problems arise during the development of software and systems; but that is why the SDP evolved. The disciplined approach of the SDP, if followed, systematically identifies what job needs to be programmed and the risks associated with that work, and requires that programming and testing practices adjust to be more or less stringent depending on that degree of risk. If the SDP needed to give this degree of control over the project was not enforced or followed, then demonstrating reasonable care may be very difficult since project and risk management control cannot be demonstrated.

QUESTIONS TO ASK TO ENSURE THAT REASONABLE CARE HAS BEEN TAKEN

The rest of this discussion will focus on a series of questions that a software or system project manager should be able to answer and show evidence of, as needed, to defend the company against a charge of software or system liability. These same questions, regardless of threats of liability, also should be asked to determine whether an IT project was under the control of corporate management.

These questions follow the logical flow of the generally accepted SDP phases and give special attention to those phases of the SDP where testing occurs. The questions and associated narrative focus on the types of documents needed to show evidence that an SDP activity actually occurred. Such documentation must be in a form that describes how the system and software works, must be usable by other than the "creator" of the document, and must allow reconstruction of SDP activities for audit purposes.

QUESTIONS: Who, from the customer/user's organization, participated in the definition of the software or system requirements? Were all parties to be "impacted" by the system represented?

Can it be proven?

DISCUSSION: Depending on the nature and complexity of the application, many "stakeholders" have an operational, legal, audit, security, management, employee, customer, and public interest in the software or system to be built. They must participate or be represented in the definition of requirements and concur with those requirements if the developer is to know what to design, program, test, and deliver.

QUESTIONS: Were quality characteristics defined as a set of specifications further describing the functional business requirements of the software/system? Did the stakeholders reach a consensus concerning how satisfaction of each quality characteristic would be measured?

Can it be proven?

DISCUSSION: Without a clear and concise understanding of how the business requirements of the new software and system are going to be measured, the developer does not have the specification information necessary to design and program the system. Without this vital customer/user acceptance information, the developer has no realistic criteria against which to test the design of the system or the program code.

QUESTIONS: How was feasibility for this project determined? Was a formal feasibility analysis required of the SDP that was used? Were the deliberations concerning technical, operational, and economic feasibility documented? Was a project risk analysis performed on the solution that survived the feasibility study? This study focuses on the business and technical implementation problems that may pose risk to the project's successful completion.

*Can documentation be produced
that reflects this thought process?*

DISCUSSION: A majority of "reasonable care" questions that can arise are answered by the analysis that was done to select the project's technical solution and the strategy for managing the effort. Solutions that were not feasible were not by definition capable of being implemented successfully. Selection of a high-risk solution may cast doubts on the wisdom of proceeding with the project and the competence of the management team running the project.

QUESTIONS: How was the extent of testing for this project determined? Was the rigor of testing determined by an examination of application risk to the business or customer, or was it based on information sensitivity and privacy issues? Was the degree of testing considered reasonable by industry practice regarding similar systems?

Can documentation be produced that reflects this thought process?

QUESTIONS: How were computer system security and internal controls for this type of application system determined? Was a formal assessment performed? Did auditors consult on controls to use to prevent, detect, reconstruct, and/or recover from breaches of security and system integrity? Do these controls extend to the workplace with its manual procedures?

Was the analysis and decision process documented?

DISCUSSION: The answer to the last two questions requires the performance of some type of computer security and internal controls analysis directed at the application to be built. This analysis should have been conducted by taking into account the critical nature of the application, the sensitivity of the system's information, and the susceptibility of the application to possible fraud, abuse, and breaches of confidentiality. To do this, all stakeholders to the definition of system requirements should have had input to the risk analysis to include computer security experts and audit specialists.

QUESTIONS: What systems development process (SDP) was followed for the project in question? Were the managers, analysts, and programmers responsible for project well versed in the sequence and importance of each phase of the SDP? Were they trained in the SDP?

Can it be proven?

QUESTIONS: Does company policy and the SDP require the generation of a formal plan and budget for the construction of the software/system in question? Did this plan and budget undergo a formal review? Is there a process for modifying the plan and budget as needed?

Does a documented plan exist?

QUESTIONS: Did the SDP incorporate periodic review points where work on the project was validated against the requirements for the software/system? Were these reviews conducted? Did the customer/user participate in the reviews? When omissions, errors, or necessary changes were discovered and corrective action taken, were these immediately reflected in the documentation of the system?

Can it be proven?

QUESTIONS: Did management of the software/system effort conduct periodic quality reviews of work products from the project for technical correctness and to affirm that sound design and programming practices were being followed? Did these reviews include a reevaluation of the testing criteria to be used later in the project?

Can it be proven?

DISCUSSION: It is important to demonstrate that the development project was well supervised. An integral part of all SDPs are the project review points where "progress against the plan" is examined to determine appropriateness and correctness of preceding work products. Evidence of having conducted these reviews is essential to claiming that reasonable care was taken during the execution of this project.

QUESTIONS: How was the continuity of the software/system development team maintained? How was knowledge of the design requirements, program status, and the testing and acceptance criteria passed from one team member to another? On large projects, how were the many ongoing development, change, and test activities accounted for and kept in sync? Were all activities documented and coordinated?

Can it be proven?

DISCUSSION: Again, the need to demonstrate sufficient management control over the project is essential to claiming that reasonable care was taken in the development of the software/system in question. Configuration management (CM) is an essential element of any SDP if control is to be maintained and be demonstrable. Without CM, medium- to large-size projects will quickly lose their integrity and confusion will reign.

QUESTIONS: Was there a quality assurance function operating during development of this software/system? Was it involved during the early phases of the project to ensure that all aspects of a quality product were addressed? What national or international standards (i.e., ISO 9000 series) constituted the benchmark for quality assurance? Did the people responsible for quality assurance work independently of the development team and the team's management? Did any outside reviews take place of the software/system while it was under development?

Can documentary proof be provided that quality assurance was performed on this project?

QUESTIONS: As requirements changed or were refined and modified, how were they managed to ensure that unexpected adverse impacts did not occur to the software or system under development? What policies and procedures existed to prevent a programmer from making a change to the software or system without proper analysis?

DISCUSSION: Software/system projects are very difficult to manage. Most SDPs and project management methods provide techniques for disciplined management of the effort. All too often, however, they are not utilized and programmers are given too much latitude to determine for themselves what they will and will not do while working on the project. To show that "reasonable care" was exercised, it must be clearly evident that the analysts and programmers were under management supervision.

*Can documentation be produced that records all changes to
the work as the work progressed?*

QUESTIONS: Did the schedule for development allot sufficient time for testing? How was the testing strategy determined? For example, was the application's sensitivity analyzed? Was the degree of risk posed by improper functioning of the application determined? Was the extent of testing determined by this degree of risk?

*Can documentation be produced that links the test strategy
to a determination of sensitivity risk?*

QUESTIONS: How was the testing effort managed for this project? What national or international standards or guidelines were used to guide the testing effort? Were any industry-unique or regulatory testing requirements used to direct the testing effort? Were the testing methods employed consistent with those used by similar companies testing similar software and systems?

*Can evidence be produced that required standards
and guidelines were followed?*

DISCUSSION: Adequate and sufficient testing will form the first line of defense against any charge of liability. Even though the existence of bugs in software and systems are accepted by unknowing customers as the way things are, the software company may be required, as the "expert," to do whatever was necessary to deliver quality software and systems given the state of the software engineering art and the criticality and risk of the function being supported by the software. This is why the criticality of the software and system under development to the business or customer was examined. Highly critical software and systems require more stringent testing that do more mundane and less important applications. The developer must be able to show that the complexity of tests and the time allotted to testing was commensurate with the risk posed to the company should the software or system fail.

QUESTIONS: As testing progressed, how were defects and corrective changes managed? Does all subsequent software and systems documentation reflect such changes? Do test plans and test data reflect such changes? Were all changes during testing and subsequent reprogramming analyzed for security, internal controls, and audit implications?

Can it be proven?

QUESTIONS: Was all software/systems documentation kept current throughout the development effort and not just fabricated at the end of the project? Were any corners cut either in testing or in documentation in order to "get the code out the door"?

Can it be proven that shortcuts were not taken?

QUESTIONS: Regarding customer/user acceptance of the software/system, did the SDP and project manager require customer acceptance signatures after each major development review point and after final system test? Do signatures exist reflecting concurrence by the security, audit, and legal stakeholders that the software and system satisfy their requirements?

Does documentation exist?

What assurances can be given to the board and to business owners that a software and system liability challenge can be defended against?

SUGGESTED READINGS

Baskerville, R. *Designing Information Systems Security.* Chichester, United Kingdom: John Wiley & Sons, 1988.

Beizer, B. *The Frozen Keyboard: Living with Bad Software.* Blue Ridge Summit, PA: TAB Books, 1988.

Birrel, N. D., and M. A. Ould. *A Practical Handbook for Software Development.* Cambridge, United Kingdom: Cambridge University Press, 1985.

Boehm, B. W. *Software Engineering Economics.* Englewood Cliffs, NJ: Prentice Hall, 1981.

Boehm, B. W., J. T. Brown, H. Kaspar, M. Lipow, G. J. MacLeod, and M. J. Merrit. *The Characteristics of Software Quality.* North-Holland, 1978.

Braithwaite, T. *The Power of IT: Maximizing Your Technology Investment.* Milwaukee, WI: ASQ Quality Press, 1996.

Braithwaite, T. *Information Service Excellence Through TQM.* Milwaukee, WI: ASQ Quality Press, 1994.

Charette, R. N. *Application Strategies for Risk Analysis.* New York: Mc-Graw-Hill, 1990.

Charette, R. N. *Software Engineering Risk Analysis and Management.* New York: McGraw-Hill, 1989.

DeMarco, T., and T. Lister. *Peopleware: Productive Projects and Teams.* New York: Dorset House, 1999.

Dijkstra, E. W. *The Science of Programming.* Englewood Cliffs, NJ: Prentice Hall, 1981.

Drucker, P. *Managing for the Future.* New York: Truman Talley Books, 1992.

Eason, K. *Information Technology and Organization Change.* London: Taylor and Francis, 1992.

Fagan, M. E. Design and Code Inspections to Reduce Errors in Program Development. *IBM Systems Journal* 15, No.3:182–211, 1976.

Heider, J. *The Tao of Leadership.* New York: Bantam Books, 1985.

Highsmith, J. A. *Adaptive Software Development.* New York: Dorset House, 1999.

ISO 9000-3. Quality Management and Quality Assurance Systems: Supply and Maintenance of Software. Geneva, Switzerland: International Organization for Standardization, 1991.

Leffingwell, D., and D. Widrig. *Managing Software Requirements: A Unified Approach.* New York: Addison-Wesley, 1999.

Minasi, M. *The Software Conspiracy: Why Software Companies Put Out Faulty Products, How They Hurt You, and What You Can Do About It.* New York: McGraw-Hill, 1999.

Mandell, S. *Computer, Data Processing and the Law.* St. Paul, MN: West Publishing Company, 1984.

Martin, J., and C. McClure. *Structured Techniques for Computing.* Englewood Cliffs, NJ: Prentice Hall, 1985.

McCabe, T. J., and G. G. Schulmeyer. *System Testing Aided by Structured Analysis: A Practical Experience.* IEEE Transactions on Software Engineering SE-11, no. 9:917–921, 1985.

Neumann, P. G. *Computer Related Risks.* New York, ACM Press, 1995.

Optner, S. L. Systems analysis for business management. Englewood Cliffs, NJ: Prentice Hall, 1968.

Ould, M. A. *Strategies for Software Engineering: The Management of Risk and Quality.* New York: John Wiley & Sons, 1990.

Perry, W. *A Standard for Testing Application Software.* Boston: Auerbach Publishers, 1990.

Royer, T. C. *Software Testing Management: Life on the Critical Path.* Englewood Cliffs, NJ: Prentice Hall, 1993.

Schindler, M. *Computer-Aided Software Design.* New York: John Wiley & Sons, 1990.

Sherer, S. A. *Software Failure Risk: Measurement and Management.* New York: Plenum Press, 1992.

Townsend, R. *Further Up the Organization.* New York: Harper and Row, 1984.

Walton, M. *The Deming Management Method.* New York, Perigee Books, 1992.

Weinberg, G. M. *Quality Software Management: Systems Thinking.* New York: Dorset House, 1992.

Yourdon, E. *Structured Walkthroughs.* New York: Yourdon Press, 1979.

Yourdon, E. *Death March.* Englewood Cliffs, NJ: Prentice Hall, 1997.

Yourdon, E. *Managing the Structured Techniques.* Englewood Cliffs, NJ: Prentice Hall, 1989.

INDEX